This book is dedicated to all the Pirates - who stuck with the team lowest level of football seen

CW00522359

INTRODUC

Welcome to the pulsating story of Bristol Rovers' 2014-15 promotion season, as chronicled through the weekly meanderings I had published on the Bristol Post web site. It's one heck of a ride, and I'll try not to spoil it by revealing the ending...

Ok, I'll admit it. As the Spring hit us and Rovers became a relatively well-oiled machine, I did begin to have this book in the back of my mind. I had put a lot of time and effort into my weekly articles (and actually managed to keep them weekly) so became internally committed to collating them together, sprinkling in some extras, and baking it into a big fat Gas pie. BURP. Then all I needed was Rovers to get promotion as no-one was going to be interested in a 'so near, yet so far' hard luck story were they?

If you've not read any of my articles before, what can you expect from this book?

On a physical level you will encounter 55 articles which are ENTIRELY unedited from what was written at the time (no hindsight for me; I will take my bad calls on the chin and accept any accolades to my heart), 16 pages of photos (mainly contributed by my fellow fans), basic details of each match, QI stats, and the odd special feature. On a higher plain you will find Hermann Hesse, Howard Hodgkin, Stuart Taylor's beard, Ice-T, Orwell, Dickins, Einstein, Gandhi, Vaughan Jones, Sham 69, and even Moussa Dagnogo.

I had no remit, except to write about BRFC, and the Bristol Post let me write basically anything I liked. I self censored myself of course and tried to remain relatively positive, patient and forgiving; not my natural traits. I felt my voice was genuine as, to para-phrase Week 17, I had no axe to grind and no baggage of being involved with Rovers or any supporters groups at any level, ever. I will also never be anyone's lap dog, and I will not pander to the loudest voice nor ignore the down trodden whimper from the gutter. I'm not a sports reporter so I didn't kick every ball for the readers after each match, and I'm not a businessman so I wasn't unduly caught up in which moneyed man (it is always a man) had bought his way onto the Board of Directors so he could take decisions that us fans should rightfully be taking ourselves.

I am just an experienced terrace fan who loves to write, likes to analyse, studied history and endeavours to dish up what my brother deliciously described as his 'five a day of culture'. I hope YOU enjoy the result.

THIS COPY IS NUMBER 266 OF A SIGNED LIMITED EDITION OF 462 COPIES

Please send any feedback to me at -
hello@awaythegas.org.uk

Martin Bull

CONTENTS

The end… of 'non-league Rovers' - thankfully

FOREWORD

BY JAMES MCNAMARA

BRISTOL ROVERS WRITER FOR THE BRISTOL POST

May 3rd, 2014 is a date that will be indelibly inked on the minds of Bristol Rovers supporters forever.

Instead of contemplating a lazy summer to recover from what had been a long hard winter following Bristol Rovers around the country (with very little success to show for it!) once the final whistle sounded at the Memorial Stadium on that fateful day, everyone associated with the football club was considering a trip into the unknown.

As angry supporters congregated under Box 1 to remonstrate with those immediately charged with being the architects of such heart-wrenching downfall, the future looked bleak. Martin had contacted the Post only eight days previously to arrange to start his blog, thinking next seasons analysis would be on yet another below-par League Two campaign.

I was considering the logistical nightmares of operating out of rudimentary non-league press boxes at far-flung and less-than-alluring outposts. That had certainly not been part of the plan when I first considered a career in sports journalism. I mean, where is Braintree, even?

For supporters, however, their fears were different. Was it the end? Perhaps statements such as those which flooded the forums in the hours and days that followed the worst day in the club's history may have been a little over-dramatic.

Yet supporters of Stockport County and Chester City may have met such out-pouring of anguish with sage nods of their heads. It had been over a decade since a club relegated from the Football League had bounced back at the first attempt. The likes of Grimsby Town, Lincoln City and Wrexham provided living proof that the weeks and months that were to follow would probably be some of the toughest that supporters of Bristol Rovers would ever have to endure.

Through Martin's weekly updates, Post readers were offered the chance to follow the feelings of anger, despair, hope and, finally, elation that encapsulated an unforgettable 12 months, through the words of a long time supporter.

It was an enjoyable journey – and who could forget the highs and lows that came with it? Early defeats at Altrincham and Braintree Town that were met with derision; the gritty 1-0 win at home against Telford that Darrell Clarke believes saved his job; the manager's infamous 'negativity' rant two days after an angry supporter tried to board the team bus following a 0-0 draw at Alfreton Town.

What about the amazing away support that forced a lock out at Woking? Who could forget Darrell's sing-song in a pub on the Gloucester Road that made headlines in Grimsby? Then, of course, there was that one swish of Lee Mansell's boot that brought the journey to an end in glorious circumstances at Wembley.

What a season.

Would I want to do it again? Probably not, but, I'm sure that 2014/15 will live long in the memory of Rovers supporters far and wide.

I'm pleased, then, that Martin has collated his meanderings from what was, at times, a nail-biting roller coaster ride and decided to 'Print that *******' for posterity.

Enjoy

WEEK ONE - SORRY, THE SYSTEM IS DOWN

PUBLISHED ON TUESDAY 6TH MAY 2014

What an inauspicious time to start a new Rovers blog!

I was fully expecting to write a piece about how any 'celebrations' after a dull draw with Mansfield had to be seen as pure relief, and not any endorsement of another dire season following Rovers.

The minds of Gasheads are currently filled with anger, depression, blame, embarrassment and anxiety about next season (already).

94 years in the league down the drain. But we'll dust ourselves down and be ready to go again in August.

Whilst it is very tempting to minutely analyse this last game (two thuds on the crossbar whilst Mansfield's goal goes in off the post, no fit full backs left at the club, and an inept Rovers free kick going out by the corner flag on the other side of the pitch) it would only be a case of sweeping the 45 other results under the carpet. A team doesn't go down on one performance.

Whilst I don't wish to dwell on 'blame', and certainly not individual denigration, the wider lessons of this season must be realised and never repeated.

We never fundamentally addressed a lack of goals from strikers, nor a far-reaching lack of pace and width in the squad or the formations. Pace causes problems to even the best defenders.

When you don't have a talented team, you coach them in a simple, clear system that plays to what little strengths you may be able to dredge up. You then repeat this ad nauseam on the training ground until your squad is enhanced. Mansfield (only seven points above us before the match and in their own mini-slump) had a system, and worked it well. They cleared their lines with long, wide, accurate balls. It almost guarantees a throw in two-thirds of the way up the pitch and time to regroup. Their wide men were by no means lofty donkeys though; they worked it inside effectively and danger-ously, and were comfortable if they got it to feet. Rochdale were similar, and even more skilled.

Our system has been down nearly all season and it never got rebooted by our usual new managerial bounce around the New Year.

The majority of our players simply aren't comfortable on the ball. A trained monkey could whack a ball as soon it got it...probably. It's been like watching a carpenter with a phobia of wood. Contrast our collective lack of self-belief, and in some cases, basic skills, to Mansfield's Anthony Howell, a dynamo with an engine, a tackle, AND hungry for the ball.

Rovers have dwelt on the defensive side of the game, especially in midfield. Although emerging young players such as Ollie Clarke, Seanan Clucas, and Tom Lockyer coped admirably this season, in a variety of roles, none could be mistaken for creative players and they didn't provide even one assist between them during 103 appearances. John-Joe O'Toole may be our valued top scorer, but even he didn't provide an assist until his 46th game.

Of course there are many more lessons to be learnt, and much minutia that could potentially be analysed, but if we can have a system, a pinch of pace, half a cup of width, and a bushel of basic skill, we might just stand a chance sometime this decade.

Print That Season!

Published in the Independent Peoples' Republic of Wiltshire by shellshock publishing

Copyright 2015 © Martin Bull, and James McNamara for his foreword.

First Edition - ISBN 978-0-9554712-8-5

Print Management by Sam Martin at TU Ink - www.tuink.co.uk

TU Ink are specialists in managing print projects for Trade Unions so I am very happy to use them for all my print needs and feel I am doing my little bit to help them continue to support Trade Unions.

The author (Martin Bull) asserts his moral right to be identified as the author of this work. The author has also had some nasty tropical diseases, slept in a hedge and fallen in a hole like an idiot, and probably doesn't wish to be identified for any of those.

The author/publisher apparently should also add some standard guff in here about 'all rights reserved', whatever that means. Ok. Please don't nick stuff from this mint book like. Instead, please contact the editor and bribe him with proper cider (not dirty apples), and he'll probably do anything you ask.

This book was NOT printed in China, and hopefully none from shellshock publishing ever will be, despite tempting prices. This book was actually printed in lovely Aberystwyth, by Cambrian Printers, a nice old independent printer.

WEEK TWO - MOURNING HAS BROKEN

PUBLISHED ON TUESDAY 13TH MAY 2014

The unofficial period of relegation mourning at Rovers is now over and the gloves are off.

The club swiftly produced their list of retained players and as expected nearly everyone who is out of contract has been allowed to leave. There are few surprises and that's exactly what most Gasheads wanted, and what I feel Darrell Clarke needed so he can stamp his own hallmarks on the squad and implement the tactics he desires.

Fans of course are still furious about the relegation and how, as usual, none of the decision makers or senior staff have resigned or been told to sign on. Turkeys don't vote for Christmas do they.

At least the elephant in the room has been told to pack its trunk and leave the circus. I had always felt apprehensive at the prospect of Darrell Clarke and John Ward trying to work together on transfer dealings. Darrell has made it very clear that he wants pace in the team, a more expansive approach, and the use of grass rather than the sky. Yet John Ward was increasingly considered a dinosaur by most fans, and his refusal to play with pace and width, and recruit any strikers who played off the shoulder of the last defender, suggested a clash of cultures not seen since my parents didn't approve of my Nik Kershaw haircut in the 1980's.

Tumbleweed has greeted the decisions taken so far. They were so obvious that they cannot be considered part the radical review we've been promised.

The Board have explained this burnt offering to the Gods by pointing the finger at fiscal belt tightening, but using the word 'sacked' simply doesn't tie up with the public explanation given by Mr.Higgs. I dearly hope that behind this rotten facade there has been a sincere acknowledgement that there was also a clear footballing rationale for this sacrifice.

The new elephant in the room though is whether Darrell Clarke needs help identifying suitable players or doing the 'boring' bits of football management. I like what I've seen of DC so far and think he could well become a popular and successful figure at Rovers, but I do worry if he really knows enough about potential players to be able to purchase at least half a squad all in one go and then get them playing effectively together within months. Paul Buckle anyone?

Even worse Rovers have a worrying history of losing their best players just after the season has already started; a situation that would test the fleet footedness of even the most experienced scout or manager.

Meanwhile, amidst this relative status quo, the two so-called 'Fans Directors' remain on the Board, foraging on crumbs from the biscuit platter of affluent businessmen. Given that Nick Higgs owns a clear majority (52%) of Bristol Rovers (1883) Ltd, I see very little point in them being there, adrift amongst the corporate testosterone. They are mere flies on the Boardroom wall. The whole state of affairs reminds me of the well known doggerel during Richard III's reign, 'The cat, the rat and Lovell our dog, rule all England under the hog'. The writer of this, William Collingbourne, was hung, drawn and quartered for his dissenting appraisal of a feudal clique.

I am surprised they haven't considered their own positions at the top table. One of them even had the temerity to tell fans to "pull together", as if 4,300 Gasheads at the last two away games, and 18,000 at the last two home games, wasn't already 'pulling together'. They do not represent the fans. They represent a few members of the Supporters Club who voted for them. If they had any dignity they would step away from the board until they are given any genuine clout, and until the gang of six begin to compassionately care about the average Rovers fan.

I'm sick and tired of us supporters taking the blame yet again for corporate and footballing failure.

The mourning is over, the gloves are off, the time has come to vacate the trough.

WEEK THREE - FOOT IN MOUTH DISEASE

PUBLISHED ON WEDNESDAY 21ST MAY 2014

When asked to name the largest sports stadium in the world you may think of an American football stadium, the MCG, or even the Azteca Stadium (once the sardonic nickname of Twerton Park). In reality the Rungnado First of May Stadium in Pyongyang, the capital of austere North Korea, has a mind bending capacity of 150,000, although given North Korea's showy displays of phoney togetherness I wouldn't be surprised if it is in fact a 5-a-side pitch made to look monumental by the use of ginormous mirrors and weapons grade cling film.

Whilst on a stadium tour there a well travelled friend of mine saw a huge sign that read 'Home of the Invincible Indomitable Indestructible Insuperable North Korean Football Team'. As he got closer he then saw in small letters added underneath, 'Twinned with Bristol Rovers F.C.'.

Ok, that's not true, but there was certainly a whiff of autocracy in the air last week at the Mem, as the only matter to publicly come out from 'the most important Board Meeting in our history', was, without warning, an immediate closure of the Fan's Forum on the official BRFC web site.

A lot on the forum was good, including some excellent analysis and statistics, bountiful witty banter, and the Fan's Forum Supporters Club (FFSC) which in barely more than a year not only put £7,500 in the club's coffers, focusing on sponsorship of young players, but also provided much needed camaraderie amongst its almost 200 members.

As with most forums, the down side was tittle-tattle, hearsay, disagreements, and just plain incivility at times.

It is unusual for a football club to host and moderate a forum about itself, especially one with over 10,000 members, and regularly getting up to 1,000 people using it during a game, so if the closure statement had solely pointed that fact out, and then given users a week to rescue any of their writings and contacts from it, BRFC could probably have metaphorically shredded the file and erased it from the history books without any fuss.

But for many years there has been a worryingly defensive and taciturn attitude at Rovers, and it seems to stem from our dear leader at the very top.

I admire Nick Higgs for his construction expertise and the UWE Stadium project, but boy does he not look comfortable when questioned about anything of greater magnitude than whether the milk should go into the teacup first, or after the water and the tea bag. Maybe it is just the media shyness of an average human being but even on the official BRFC interviews he looks uncomfortable and gives off an impression that even meagre scraps of information need to be wrenched out like rotten teeth.

Communication from the club is at best amateur, or at worst, plain dictatorial.

So barely a week after promising a top to toe investigation into the whole putrid setup, the Board (including the so-called Fans Directors) knowingly decided it was a wise move to release a statement accusing the fans (yet again the fans...) of forcing them to close it, and then telling Gasheads to "follow" on twitter instead, where they can "receive" official information. This sounded more like Orwell's 'newspeak', or Adam Susan's proclamations about 'V', than a two way dialogue.

The web site headline wrote that they had decided to "suspend" the Fans Forum, whereas the by-line read that it was "closed with immediate effect". The week before John Ward had been "sacked" (even though the reason given was purely financial), whereas a few days later three back room staff were going to "leave the club". Are these perplexing differences in language calculated or just plain shoddy?

You really couldn't make up what happened next.

In an effort to soothe the long suffering supporters the club announced a 'Fans Forum' for July. The small print added that it was only for Season Ticket holders and Supporters Club members. Doh! If the opinions of all fans are equal, some seem to be more equal than others.

Everything at the moment is one step forward, five steps back.

I really do not want to be focusing on this flotsam. I have a dozen half written articles about BRFC football issues being held up in the pipeline. But the Board put their foot in their mouths so often they must have veruccas in their windpipes, and to side step these crucial issues now would be fiddling whilst Horfield burnt.

WEEK FOUR – HE WHO SUPS WITH THE DEVIL NEEDS A LONG SPOON

PUBLISHED ON TUESDAY 27TH MAY 2014

The old story goes that the blues guitarist Robert Johnson sold his soul to the Devil at a crossroads on a dusty road. This Faustian pact gave him a masterly ability with the guitar, but in return the Devil got his soul and an early death, establishing him as the first well known member of the '27 Club' [talented musicians who died aged just 27].

I'm not sure where the club we support sold its soul, and what they got for it (it certainly wasn't success on the pitch), but I wonder if the club made an injudicious pact with the Devil, or has upset some mighty powerful Gods in its time?

Let's be honest, Rovers have flirted with relegation too many times, as this new century has been riddled with disasters. Several times Rovers drew away from a potential drop, but the club never seemed to deeply meditate on how close demotion had truly been and how to make lasting changes that will prevent it actually happening one season.

Like Icarus, the club ignored fatherly advice and flew too close to the sun. Both realised too late that they had little more than wax and old feathers to hold their flights of fancy together. Does anyone remember the Five Year Plan to get into the Championship? We'd be lucky now to be able to formulate a workable plan to make an emergency rain hat out of an old newspaper.

In nine seasons of bottom tier football the Gas were consistently no-where near the top half of the table by mid-season, and thus had little chance of a getting out of that division (the right way at least). In fact our average position on New Year's Eve was a lowly 17th. That should have rung alarm bells at Board level more thunderous than Big Ben itself. How can you have a successful team if you constantly run the first half of a Marathon struggling along in a fancy dress clown outfit three sizes too big for you?

Rovers' first ever season in the Fourth Tier (2001/02) was the start of a brace of disastrous years, the severity of which took most of us by surprise after a riotously enjoyable decade in 1990's. Gerry Francis's return proved the old adage to 'never go back' and the expectation of an immediate return to the Third was far too optimistic. Looking back, we (the fans) can't really be blamed for our optimism, or our slight narcissism. BRFC had never been in the bottom tier before and we all felt there was no obvious impediment to a return to familiar territory soon. The club were still getting higher crowds than nearly everyone in the bottom tier, and were still raising money from selling talent.

We infamously finished 23rd that season on a paltry 45 points, but those were the days (the last year to be exact) when only one team was relegated, and as Halifax Town were a basket case, relegated as early as April Fools Day, there was no real pressure to get us out of the mire. In fact the opposite was happening, as the only jewel left in the decaying casket, Nathan Ellington, was sold on transfer deadline day for £1.2m to Wigan, a team Gasheads had been watching only a season earlier and who were still just a mid-table Third Tier team at that point. They however now had a rich backer. We had Bradshaw's Snack Box.

Uncle Ray Graydon's first season, in 2002/03, was barely healthier. The team were constantly in the bottom five from early November onwards and were only 'rescued' by the most dramatic Easter resurrection since a certain fellow two Millennia previously. Andy Rammell may have only played seven games for us & scored only in those crucial three wins, but he'll never need to buy a drink again in our beautiful city. We finished merely three points off relegation, and would have been goners without even half of those 10 points from the last four games.

We were at our lowest ebb. I don't feel the club, or us fans, have ever properly recovered from those three seasons from 2000 to 2003, despite the temporary improvement thereafter.

2003/04 was a minor miracle as we only flirted with relegation for a few weeks in March, before finishing fifteenth. The bore fests of Ian Atkins in 2004/05 (rising from seventeenth to twelfth on the final game of the season) and 2005/06 (another twelfth place finish), were essentially the stability we needed and he put in place the building blocks of what was to become the most unlikely promotion in our history, especially considering that we were still slumbering in sixteenth place in mid-March 2007.

Since the heart warming sojourn in the Third Tier from 2007 to 2011, the club has blindly tumbled down more stairs than a South African prisoner in an Apartheid era detention centre.

Those final three league seasons are of course still fresh in the memory. Managerial changes provided the impetus for scrambles away from serious trouble two seasons in a row, but that third season caught us. No [proper] managerial change, and the most embarrassing relegation in our long history.

BRFC has to learn from this disastrous 21st Century. Like Robert Johnson, we are at a life changing crossroads. I just hope the Board of Directors are finally going to pick the right direction.

WEEK FIVE – CATCH 44

PUBLISHED ON TUESDAY 3RD JUNE 2014

What's Catch 44 I hear you ask?

It's Catch 22, but twice as fiendishly problematic.

Last week we had our first definite news of whether any of our players are staying or leaving, and as we are now into June I suspect we may hear more news this week.

To borrow a Clash song, the subject of 'should I stay or should I go?' is as knotty as a labyrinthine contract drawn up by Wycombe Wanderers.

You have to question the ambition of any players, except maybe the young lads, who would want to stay at Rovers now that we're in non-league. And surely we don't really want to retain any players with such a lack of ambition or self belief? But we need some players. If they did all leave there will be trouble, and if they stay it will be double.

That's Catch 22.

So, as a logical progression from Catch 22, if a player does stay you are left doubting if inflated wages or their own lack of ability to play at a higher level could be the reason they haven't left? And then you would naturally ask yourself why we would want players like that and what negative influence this state of affairs could have on the team, especially on new, hungrier signings, whose bellies aren't full and whose pay is lower. Players, and agents, talk. They get to know what each other earns.

That's Catch 44.

Maybe I'm being too harsh and have forgotten to factor loyalty into this equation?

Unfortunately loyalty only seems to work one-way in football at the moment. If a player has a contract, his club will loyally support him, even when injured, under investigation by higher powers, or going through a personal nadir. Conversely, if a player wishes to turn his back on the club, it seems he can quite easily engineer a move away and suffer no consequences for it, except maybe a few choice songs from the terraces if they ever dare return.

In a week where Rickie Lambert has moved to one of the most successful clubs in the world, and will be on a plane to Brasil, it reminds me of the old adage that you need to keep your best players in order to progress. Fortunately it seems like a few of our best players are genuinely pleased to stay and fight, including Steve Mildenhall, although I suspect an attractive salary may still be a factor in any evaluations made.

Slightly bizarrely we had two players named in the Professional Footballers' Association (PFA) League Two Team of the Season, whereas all the other nine were from promoted teams. One of course was the brilliant Michael Smith. The other was John-Joe O'Toole. Are these awards a source of pride, or did they just highlight the overall under achievement at Rovers?

Although Gasheads expected JJ to solicit a move away, and take his questionable mind set with him, I think we were shocked that we didn't even receive a bag of magic beans for him as some naïve yokel had allowed a 'get out of jail free' card to infiltrate his portly contract. That just about sums up the confidence he had in us and why we should never have appeared so desperate to give him the golden egg the goose had laid. As one twitterer remarked "helped take you down but doesn't have the guts to stay and help you back up".

A test case in loyalty (from either side; our club is equally dis-loyal to us fans if it constantly flogs its finest prospects) may be Ryan Brunt. I sense Gasheads would be irritated if the alleged interest in Ryan Brunt led to a transfer after his infinitesimal contribution to the side last season. He didn't score a solitary goal, although he never looked wholly fit to me and later had a succession of operations. He showed his potential the previous season though, and as long as his injuries don't lead to another Dominic 'sick note' Blizzard scenario, I think his heady mix of strength and skill could tear defences apart in the Conference.

WEEK SIX – 40 YEARS IN THE WILDERNESS

PUBLISHED ON WEDNESDAY 11TH JUNE 2014

Most readers will probably know the Biblical story of the baby Moses left in his basket amongst the reeds of the River Nile, and you may also recall the older Moses in front of the burning bush, where he receives his calling in life to lead the Israelites home to a better life.

But if you can conjure up what happened in the 80 years between the alleged events, a Sunday School swot badge awaits you.

Well, he grew up and became a man in the Pharaoh's household, surrounded by worldly riches and the aroma of ultimate power, but as a mid-life crisis approached he abruptly realised that his adoptive land was persecuting his birth people, the Hebrews. After slaying an Egyptian tormentor (a lot of slaying went on in these days) he fled to the wilderness where he stayed for 40 years.

What on earth has this got to do with Bristol Rovers?

Well, no-one ever said it was going to be easy being a Rovers fan. We didn't sign up expecting glory. We could easily be Liverpool fans and 'support' them via the TV.

No-one ever said we wouldn't be forced into a 'eureka' moment where we finally stood up and fought for our brethren, after years of submission to our so-called benevolent masters.

And no-one ever said we wouldn't have our time in the wilderness; although we dearly hope it isn't as long as 40 years.

Like Moses, these wilderness years will prepare us to endure the discourage-ments, disenchantment, and hardships we will encounter, and to handle with patience, humility, long-suffering, self-control and strength the multitude of problems a great renaissance will present.

As we wait for any meaningful progress from the Boards 'top to toe' review, several supporters meetings are at least taking place for Rovers fans. None of these meetings will be perfect but all will give some chance to have a say and to be constructive about our future. One meeting is arranged by the official Supporters Club where maybe they will hopefully show that they aren't just puppets of the Board. A new Independent Supporters Club has already met and will officially launch themselves soon, and another group of fans also met together this week.

A misanthrope may suggest that splitting the fan base at this critical juncture is bad news, and that it makes 'divide and rule' easier for the powers that be. But it is important that the official Supporters Club is challenged, and surely ALL discussion is useful. Competition in life generally leads to progress.

I'm just as frustrated as you all are with our current predicament but the negativity surrounding the club has reached epic proportions, and at some point soon it surely has to stop, particularly for on-the-pitch matters.

It seems clear that Jamie White is exactly the kind of 'fox in the box' striker we need and have asked for, so I'm not sure how some Rovers fans can turn his signing into a negative. Of course he probably should have been bought a year ago, and of course Darrell Clarke now has to press forward another step and show us that he can spot good talent whom he HASN'T previously worked with, but we, the fans, need to be living in the present and we should allow ourselves at least one day of smiling amidst the melancholy.

Due to a complex contractual issue White conveniently came to us as a free transfer, but we did used to pay good money to buy the cream of the non-league crop and it will be interesting to see if the Board will put their Rickie Lambert money where their mouth is and sanction such a payment again if the right player is available to join him. Hayles, Ellington and Foster cost only £500,000 all in. And if you really want to talk about 'profit', rather than their immeasurable contribution on the pitch, then £2.7million was a sum even Del Boy would have been proud of.

No matter what mistakes go on upstairs, or even on the pitch, WE fans are the true beating heart of the club and being a Pirate / Gashead is just as much of our collective culture as anything else is in this world.

We, the fans, will endure this wilderness and we will come back stronger for it.

WEEK SEVEN – "YOU KNOW WE'RE SO VERY HUMBLE"

PUBLISHED ON THURSDAY 19TH JUNE 2014

Such were the incongruous words of Uriah Heep to David Copperfield.

I can see a little of BRFC in the obsequiousness of Heep. Over recent years we seem to have lost some of our humility. But we have a chance now to redeem ourselves.

A myriad of written and anecdotal evidence over the years has suggested that footy supporters often liked Bristol Rovers. People like quirky; singing a bizarrely depressing song from the 1930's, the only team to wear quarters, and happily calling ourselves something to do with a stinky old gas works. We had the 'Tote End', we had greyhounds and rose beds at our (rented) Stadium, we later played on a lop sided pitch at Twerton, where the fans were literally a hairs breadth from the players, and we travelled away in boisterous blue and white swathes.

We had little real success, but did help produce a long list of excellent players, who we could rarely keep hold of. Our feet were on the ground and never got too big for our Pirate boots. Previous to 2001 we were the only club in the 92 who had never been in the top tier or the Fourth Tier after its creation in 1958. We bounced around the centre quite happily. The middle of the road wasn't actually as boring as people may have expected.

As a Twerton lad I've never had much affinity with the Mem and something ominous certainly seems to have happened during our tenure here. The Board sold so much talent in the late 1990's that it became embarrassing, and it finally caught up with us as we suffered our first ever relegation to the Fourth Tier in 2001. Apart from 2007 to 2010 this new century has been a disaster, and even that heady period of success gave rise to our ultimate downfall.

The club became conceited. They talked of being a regular fixture in the Championship. Respected players were unceremoniously frozen out because they allegedly weren't good enough for League One. They paid over the odds for players who failed at teams higher than us, rather than harvesting the cream of the lower league crop. The club handed out large contracts to players with even larger waistlines, fell for agent spiel when told there were lots of other teams wanting to sign that mediocre 30 year old, and after giving Paul Trollope five years the Board then ran in completely the opposite direction and changed managers more regularly than Salisbury City get into financial strife.

I'm therefore not sure other fans like us quite so much now. Brashness and failure have jaded us, and also removed some of our sense of humour and self-deprecating demeanour.

This season though is our golden chance to be more humble again and not to expect that so-called little clubs will come to the Mem and lump it up in the air, or treat us with awe. If I had a shekel for every time I've heard Gasheads whinge that we never deserved to get beaten by, insert so-called 'small club' here, I could have bought Wycombe Wanderers a couple of contract lawyers by now.

Rather like a first week in prison, charitable fans of conference teams have been quick to educate us on what not to do in our unfamiliar new surroundings. They've advised us not to recruit a team of ex-league players, not to pay said has-beens lots of cash for failure, and most importantly not to expect anyone to care who we are or where we've been for 94 years, or for us to imagine teams will see us as their 'Man U' fixture of the season and 'raise their game' against us. Their CLUB may see our large away support as that in financial terms, especially after the loss of Luton fanatics, but the eleven on the pitch certainly won't! To players we're just A.N.Other team standing in the way of them getting an opportunity in league football and making a better life for themselves.

We should expect good quality, fast, and raw, attacking football. The idea that it's just a bunch of part-time lumpers, playing on a cabbage patch, is out-of-date. Indeed history suggests that the teams that make it out of the Conference nearly always do well in the Football League.

The Board weren't humble enough to listen to what Gulls fans told us about a certain ex-manager before we sneakily head hunted him. Let's hope we do listen to experienced non-league fans before we repeat the mistakes nearly all other relegated teams have made in the past.

Given the continued arrogance and hand washing of the Board, I feel we only have one chance to restore our reputation at the moment, and his name is Darrell Clarke. This man has a plan and he is the only one showing any humility and morals at present. His mentality of human and financial discipline, and the pursuit of hungry non-league players, is admirable for our present state.

Mark my words, Darrell will do very well somewhere.

Let's make sure it is at BRFC and that he isn't chased away by either the fans, the players or the Board.

WEEK EIGHT – THE SHOCK OF THE NEW

PUBLISHED ON TUESDAY 24TH JUNE 2014

It often feels as though the quality, and style, of football in the Conference is unfairly maligned.

One serious problem with believing that largely out-of-date view is that it can lead clubs into a false sense of security, and as focused on in last weeks column, a distinct lack of humility; both of which will almost guarantee a shock from the division of hell.

We have been told by Conference fans to generally expect good quality, fast, and raw, attacking football. Our club ought to be listening to that in order to be prepared for the shock of the new. Thankfully we have a manager who although never got a chance to manage in the Conference (as he came to us just after he got Salisbury City promoted into it), did have three very success-ful years as their manager in the two tiers immediately below the Confer-ence, and therefore certainly knows the sphere of football we are now in.

Evidence suggests that the teams that make it out of the Conference nearly always do well in the Football League, so surely they must have plenty of quality in them.

Only two teams go up, so it's even more competitive than League Two (the only league where four go up), and you truly do need the perfect season to get the sole automatic promotion slot. Indeed in the last 10 seasons exasper-ated Conference runners up have finished with a staggering average of 86 points. Wrexham once only came second despite racking up 98 points and a goal difference of +52. To add insult to injury they were then ruthlessly beaten in the play-off semi-final.

If you're still not convinced about the quality of the league, especially the fully professional clubs, take a look at the teams that have escaped from the Conference, and see where they are today. Of the last 10 teams to be promoted (barring last season as it's too early to tell), only one has since been relegated back to non-league (Torquay United), and even they enjoyed two play-off slots in their four seasons in League Two. That was more than Rovers achieved in nine long seasons in League Two.

Crawley Town and Stevenage Borough have been the two high flyers of course, coming from no league history at all and both gaining back-to-back the Conference, through League Two without stopping, and into League One. Crawley have since finished tenth and 15th in League One. Stevenage were even more successful at the start, finishing sixth in their first League One season, but then struggled for the next two, finishing 18th and then bottom. Fleetwood Town haven't been far behind as after saying goodbye to the Conference in 2012 they finished 13th and fourth in League Two, and have just been promoted again via the play-offs.

Oxford United have been consistently, if rather laboriously, strong (12th, ninth, ninth & eighth) and Burton Albion have been a real slow burning sensation (13th, 19th & 17th, but then fourth & sixth). York City are now on a roll; a difficult first season in 17th, but a late play-off slot last season via seventh position. Mansfield Town and Newport County rode some patchy form last season to finish their inaugural seasons back in the league 11th and 14th respectively. Only the phoenix from the flames (AFC Wimbledon) has consistently struggled, and also waned, finishing 16th, 20th & 20th.

If we are to stand a chance of exiting this league we need to retain the few decent players we have left, unless their salary is completely engorged for this level. With Lee Brown signing a new contract we received the first fragment of genuinely excellent news about our existing players. I very much rate Brown and when I think of the attributes I want in a player he ticks all the boxes, including my slightly eccentric one about players not posting fatuous drivel on twitter or Facebook.

It is also heartening to see that Darrell Clarke has principles when dealing with players, and as he believes that all players are replaceable at this level, Rovers won't be offering excessive wages to anyone. New contracts will also be heavily performance related, which is something I've been banging on about for ages.

Despite the bigger issues of pessimism surrounding the abysmal manner in which Rovers is run from up on high, and the tardy resolution of the Wycombe affair, I bet we have all still pencilled Saturday 9th of August in our diaries for the first game of the Conference season. No matter what gets thrown at us, football fans still want to go and watch their team. Every season, nay, every match, we still go with equal parts of expectation and trepidation. It's like an inexplicable joie de vivre cocktail. Ever time I go to the match I think it will be better than before. A few minutes after kick-off I realise it may not be, but if we didn't have that hope in our hearts I'm sure none of us would ever get off the sofa.

WEEK NINE - NEVER GO BACK

PUBLISHED ON TUESDAY 1ST JULY 2014

They say that managers should 'never go back' to a club, as the second time around is never as successful as the first.

Second time failure is not partisan and can be as high profile as Kevin Keegan at Newcastle United and Kenny Dalglish at Liverpool, or as low profile as Jim Gannon at Stockport County, every Gasheads' favourite figure of fun. Some managers even go back to two clubs, with varying degrees of success, such as Graham Taylor at Watford and Aston Villa, and Ronny Moore at Rotherham United and Tranmere Rovers.

Obviously only successful and popular managers are ever asked back, so despite a recent crop of success stories like Nigel Pearson at Leicester City and Eddie Howe at AFC Bournemouth, it's frequently going to end in tears.

BRFC of course had it with Bobby Gould and Gerry Francis, and now we've had it again with John Ward.

After leading us to 12th place in the Third Tier in 1981/82 and seventh in 1982/83, Bobby Gould moved on to Coventry City, and David Williams, who at 28 years old was not surprisingly the League's youngest manager, took us even higher, finishing fifth and then sixth. Although Bobby's second spell wasn't downright disastrous, it was a clear backward step, finishing 16th and 19th between 1985 and 1987, with survival going down to that famous last game of the season at Newport County in May 1987.

Do I really need to remind Pirates of King Gerry's first era in charge? He joined a club who didn't have a pot to pee in, and inherited Gould's brittle squad who couldn't score goals, but in the next four years we had a play-off final, a Football League Trophy final, became Third Tier Champions, and then achieved our highest League finish since 1960.

Gerry Francis's 'never go back' moment in 2001 though followed a history busting relegation, and it always felt contrived to me. It was very romantic to persuade the messiah to return but did he really want to? The temporary ascent at the start (third place in mid-September) made the fall even harder to bear, as Rovers never won again in the League and Gerry mysteriously resigned on Christmas Eve, with Rovers in 22nd place. His average of 0.95 points per League game paled into insignificance compared to his 1.58 average during 1987-1991.

Can I add Garry Thompson into this fetid mix? He was equally disastrous in both spells though, being the bread of a salmonella sandwich before and after Gerry's homecoming. Looking back you do wonder what on earth the Board were doing giving him 47 games in charge, where he produced nigh on identical results both times. His first spell (won 7, drew 5, lost 11) contributed to that earth-shattering 2001 relegation, and his second spell (won 7, drew 5, lost 12), barely six months later, would have done the same if Halifax Town weren't a basket case and it being the last season when only one club was jettisoned out of the Football League backdoor.

The eagerly anticipated Bristol Rovers Supporters Club EGM last week gave us some breaking news. John Ward, our most current 'never go back' failure and patently absent from the meeting, was entirely to blame for last season, and footy historians are invited to metaphorically put his head on a spike and display it outside the Mem, whilst our great leader in the sky summons' the plebeian hordes to gather around and eat cake.

Comments from the EGM leave you wondering what to believe, and why basic issues weren't sorted out. Why couldn't John Ward's position within the club have been VERY clear, vis-à-vis who wanted what, and what the plan was? Why make the change after the transfer window had closed when Ward asked for the change in February?

Does it matter now who is telling the tale accurately?

Not completely. They all messed up and it sounds like there was not enough honest, adult communication between ANY of them. It does make you wonder what actually happens when a Board (or the Chair) converses with a manager. Do they really 'appraise' his performance, like any boss / employee relationship, and talk of future plans and even any personal concerns, or is it just cigars, Ferrero Rocher and manly back slapping?

Every Gashead knew that Darrell Clarke was seen as a rapid replacement for at least the hands on managerial matters, so if JW made it clear he never wished to manage the entire season why not make an earlier change? JW had done admirably in 2013 but didn't automatically need to continue any further. It felt to me as though his role continued because he was in the job, rather than it being part of any logical plan. John had famously been on a train to Plymouth to talk to Argyle about being a wise old Director of Football to a young, inexperienced manager, but instead he stopped at Bristol and became a 61 year old hands-on manager here. That never made sense as anything other than a very short term plan.

I once witnessed a young man roll up to a ragbag cricket match in his white disco jeans, and after being mistaken for a serious cricketer (he was the only one with 'the kit' on you see…), was made captain.

Neither of the above decisions made any more sense than employing a monkey to take charge of a banana packing factory.

Wrong man, wrong role.

Ultimately it is the Board, including the so-called 'Fans Directors', who come out of this looking bad. They can kick a man when he's down (and absent) but the organisational buck stops with them, not the manager. They should have been more assertive in demanding to know exactly what ALL parties felt / wanted, and then found a way to give Rovers the best chance of success. That would have most probably resulted in an earlier change, and survival.

Was that too much to ask?

WEEK TEN – SLEEPING GIANT, COMATOSED BLUE WHALE

PUBLISHED ON TUESDAY 8TH JULY 2014

Catchy title for an east Asian film eh?

When I look back over 25 years supporting Rovers there have been times recently where we were regarded as a 'sleeping giant' by some, which makes you wonder what on earth we may be now, whilst ensconced in non-League? We weren't ever a 'giant' of course, but the press love sound bites and it's much catchier than 'deteriorating medium sized club with several unique features' isn't it?

If BRFC was a sleeping 'whatever' when we dropped into the Fourth Tier for the first time ever in 2001, then after nine sorry seasons of Fourth Tier footy out of the 13 seasons that followed, culminating in a further drop into non-league, we must surely now be a comatosed blue whale.

Am I stepping on toes here, and not displaying the humility I railed about a few weeks ago? No. This isn't about humility. This is about statistics. I'm not saying we currently ought to be higher than where we deservedly are (that would be arrogance), I'm merely demonstrating that our historic average position has been a lot higher, and therefore it's not conceited if Gasheads have a higher position in the back of their minds that they are comfortable with and aspire to return to ASAP. Many Gasheads CAN actually remember Bert Tann's amazing team in the 1950's, and Bill Dodgin's and Don Megson's warriors in the 1970's. And even more remember the success of the 1990's of course.

If any red lurkers who love to leave negative comments on Rovers articles have read this far down they may now be poised at their warrior keyboards to tell us that we are too big for our boots.

But it's too easy to re-write history and erroneously conclude that our success in and around the 1990's (Third Tier Champions, three Third Tier play-offs, our highest League finish since 1960 and Football League Trophy finalists) was not a true reflection of our historic position within the 92 clubs, and to insinuate that from 1989 to 2000 we were punching WELL above our weight.

We weren't.

Based on the entire 94 years of league history we should be able to commonly achieve mid-table football in the Third Tier. That is not an unreasonable ambition, and it is the one that today's manager and players, led by the Board of Directors, must put right.

It is easy for younger fans, or those not as statto'ed as I like to be, not to realise that in the 47 seasons between the resumption of League football after the Second World War (1946/47) and 1992/93, Rovers spent 19 seasons in the Second Tier, and finished in the top half of the Third Tier 20 times out of the remaining 28 seasons.

Even after relegation back to the Third Tier in 1993, exciting times followed during eight assured seasons under the tutelage of John Ward and Ian Holloway, with top half finishes in five out of the eight seasons, including two play-off appearances.

It has only been the new Century that has been riddled with disaster, and even that included a promotion, a second appearance in the Football League Trophy final, and only our third ever FA Cup quarter-final appearance.

Meaningless now of course, but they were fleeting glimpses of salvation.

Our average position over the entire 94 year stint in the Football League was tenth in the Third Tier. Since post-war, even with those nine abysmal seasons in the Fourth Tier thrown in, it was actually slightly higher, at ninth in the Third Tier. And if you want to cheat a bit, and remember just the best times, Rovers' average position from post-war to 2000 was an outstanding third in the Third Tier.

Most Rovers fans don't want to get involved in all the politics, the squabbles and the doom and gloom. They just want to watch a vaguely respectable and enthusiastic team, playing vaguely attacking footy, sing Irene alongside some good comrades, and have a bit of a laugh. Preferably all in the Third Tier of league footy. That's all most of us ask for. We appeal to the Board and the manager to get us the organisation, the players, the discipline and the correct ethos in order to return to this!

WEEK 11 - DIVIDE AND RULE

PUBLISHED ON WEDNESDAY 16TH JULY 2014

Tuesday 8th July - First Pre-season friendly

Cirencester Town 1   Bristol Rovers XI   1

Williams - 78'   D'Ath - 59'

Rovers: Craig Ross (Kane Manning, 55), Ryan Higgins, Pierce Mitchell, Danny Haile, Danny Greenslade, Dominic Thomas, Jonathan Brown (Aaron Ward-Baptiste, 46), Lawson D'Ath, Lewis Rankin (Jordan Forrester, 46), Jamie Lucas, Lewis Taaffe.

The Rovers web site added the following info - "Rovers fielded a team made up of triallists and first year pros. Goalkeeper Craig Ross is a former Cambridge United shot stopper, and the other triallists, with their former clubs in brackets, are; Ryan Higgins (Birmingham), Pierce Mitchell (Bristol City), Danny Haile (Hartpury College), Jonathan Brown (Hereford), Lawson D'Ath (Reading / Dagenham), Lewis Taaffe (Concorde Rangers), Lewis Rankin and Jordan Forrester (Coventry)."

Divide and Rule

"If the kids are united, then we'll never be divided".

So bawled the people's poet laureate, Jimmy Pursey of Sham 69.

At a time when unity is needed Rovers fans seem to be split apart even more than before. Whilst this situation may be tolerable in the short run, if it continues it may make sustained improvements at our club an even harder prospect.

We seem to be in an atypical 'divide and rule' situation, as usually it is the ruler who can be 'blamed' for shrewdly instigating divisions amongst dissenters. This time it is the fans who are voluntarily dividing themselves. Indeed the Board gave us fans the perfect chance to come together when they brusquely axed the official fans forum.

A new Bristol Rovers Independent Supporters Association (BRISA) has just been officially launched. In the longer term I suspect that this venture is the sole split in the fan base that could prove imperative for long-suffering Rovers fans. It is acutely important that the official Supporters Club is challenged, along with its all too cosy relationship with BRFC, its pillow talk partner. Competition in life generally leads to progress. BRISA will obviously never be able to compete with the Official Supporters Club as a supplier of practical fan services like away travel and ticket sales, and nor will it try to do so, but if well supported and managed fittingly it should be able to provide a strong voice of advocacy for the many frustrated Rovers fans who want the club to be run in a fit and proper manner, and to be responsive to pertinent feedback and requests from the fan base.

A separate group of fans have met together several times. This group has eloquent, visible leaders, and has garnered an impressive amount of press coverage, but hasn't plumped for a name yet.

Even the Internet forums are now split. After the Board unceremoniously disenfranchised thousands of members of the official fan's forum in May at the click of mouse button, many fans piled over to the Independent Forum which had been running, in various guises, for many years. But a new forum was soon set up, thus splitting the fan base yet again. The first chance to have all cyber space Pirates in one vessel was scuttled within a week.

This is all starting to remind me of the scene in the classic Monty Python film 'Life of Brian' when the opposition to the Romans splits into the People's Front of Judea, the Judean People's Front, the Judean Popular People's Front, and finally, the Popular Front of Judea, consisting of a lone bearded old man.

There will not be a revolution at Rovers. A company that is 52% owned by one man will rarely fall to a peasants revolt. And alas, if a substantial chink in the Boardroom armour did emerge us fans are not currently showing ourselves capable of encouraging unified, game changing, pressure on this Board. Everyone wants to be a leader; no-one wants to be a follower.

But hold on, this is democracy. Everyone should be able to say what they want, instigate different groups, set up new forums etc? Of course they can, and each individual opinion is just as valid as another, but if this variety of groups really want any chance at affecting change, rather than being comfy clubs where pretty much everyone agrees with each other, and the ones that don't quite agree are sitting on the grass outside next to the Popular Front of Judea, they have to try to come together and live within any possible differences.

The bottom line is numbers. The reason the official supporters club has even a minuscule say on the Board is because of its high membership numbers. And it has high numbers partly because the club have allowed it to offer a tangible benefit; priority purchase on scarce tickets.

It's a dreary circle of trust. Funnily enough the original meaning of a 'revolution' is precisely that; smoothly revolving from A and coming back around to A again, like the turn of a wheel, with no, or little, change.

1978 was a quiet year, with no sizeable revolts, but to the revolutionaries yet to reach maturity Sham 69's advice was apt, "They can lie to my face, but not to my heart, If we all stand together, it will just be the start".

Hardly the prose of Shakespeare, but powerful, uncomplicated words of unity.

QI STATS - TWO'S COMPANY, THREE'S A THRASHING

Rovers were the only team in the top five English football leagues who never let in more than two goals in a game during the 2014-15 season.

The only team with a lower 'Goals Against' (average per game) was Shrewsbury Town, with 31 goals in 46 games (compared to our 34 in 46 games). Chelsea and Southampton let in less goals than us overall but played far fewer games.

WEEK 12 - GIVE PEACE A CHANCE

PUBLISHED ON FRIDAY 25TH JULY 2014

Tuesday 15th July - Second Pre-season friendly

Cheltenham Town 1   Bristol Rovers 0

Harrison - 75'

Rovers: Steve Mildenhall, Ryan Higgins, Tom Lockyer, Mark McChrystal, Tom Parkes, Lee Brown, Stuart Sinclair, Lee Mansell, Ollie Clarke (Jake Gosling, 52), Matty Taylor, Ellis Harrison (Jamie White, 52).

Unused Substitutes: Aaron Ward-Baptiste, Jamie Lucas, Danny Greenslade, Dominic Thomas, Pierce Mitchell, Kieran Preston

Attendance: 767

Saturday 19th July - Third Pre-season friendly

Bath City 1   Bristol Rovers XI 0

Keary - 81'

Rovers: Kieran Preston, Ryan Higgins, Neal Trotman, Pierce Mitchell, Danny Greenslade, Ryan Broom, Dominic Thomas, Aaron Ward-Baptiste (Jamie Lucas, 58), Jake Gosling, Dan Thompson (Ellis Harrison, 53), Jamie White.

Unused Substitute: Ollie Clarke

Attendance: 837   Referee: Mr P Rees

Tuesday 22nd July - Fourth Pre-season friendly

Yeovil Town 2   Bristol Rovers 0

Leitch-Smith - 47', 55'

Rovers: Steve Mildenhall, Ryan Higgins, Lee Brown, Tom Lockyer, Mark McChrystal, Tom Parkes, Lee Mansell (Dominic Thomas, 60) (Ellis Harrison, 76), Ollie Clarke (Stuart Sinclair, 32), Ryan Brunt (Daniel Thompson, 35), Matty Taylor (Jamie White, 60), Jake Gosling.

Unused Substitutes: Neal Trotman, Kieran Preston

Attendance: 1,498, inc 289 Gas   Referee: Christopher Powell

Wednesday 23rd July - Fifth Pre-season friendly

Mangotsfield United 1   Bristol Rovers XI 1

McNab - 14'   Thomas - 39'

Rovers: Kieran Preston, Tyler Little, Danny Greenslade, Louis Ezwele, Pierce Mitchell, Jay Malpas, Chris Jones (Ryan Broom, 46), Dominic Thomas, Jamie Lucas (Aaron Ward-Baptiste, 65), Jacob Davidge (Harrison Trueman, 63).

Give Peace a Chance

Forgive my un-Rovers' like positivity but I don't understand some of the negativity surrounding our manager and our new players. Whether you call it cabin fever, sun stroke, or the continued depression from four dreadful seasons at Rovers; I call most of it plain unhelpful. Maybe it is too Utopian of me, but wouldn't it be lovely if we could peacefully welcome new players with open arms and judge them when they actually step on a blade of grass, rather than via a quick foray onto Wikipedia?

I can appreciate that some feel the managerial vacancy should have been put out to tender, but Darrell Clarke is the boss now so it would be rational to give the guy a fair chance. Darrell achieved two promotions in three seasons as a player-manager with Salisbury City, and did very well in several Cup competitions, so I've been surprised to see this labelled a tin pot achievement by some, with the logic presented being that they were a relatively big fish in a little pond. Yes, but success is never a gimme at any level of the football pyramid and numerous experienced managers and/or big budgets have failed to get 'big' teams promoted.

Darrell may 'only' have four years managerial experience, but apart from the memory that 'Ollie had zero and Gerry Francis only one disastrous season at Exeter, surely what really matters is that he DID actually achieve this success, and that many of the managerial responsibilities he obviously coped with well at The Whites, such as recruitment, contracts, training sessions, tactics, fitness, motivation, research, human dynamics, and his own relationship with his Board of Directors, will, to some degree, be similar at any level of football. A winner is a winner at any altitude.

In fact, when analysing those three seasons, gaining promotion through the play-offs both times showed immense character and a winning mentality. His team, which he was physically at the heart of, could handle pressure and never gave up. They weren't the best team in the league for either season but still dragged themselves over the finish line. In 2010/11 Clarke and Mikey Harris were thrown in the deep end after the clubs financial problems and double relegation. The Whites suffered a poor finish to the league season, yet still won the play-offs, against teams in better form than them, both of whom had already beaten them during the regular season. 2012/13 saw the opposite mode of pressure, as they had long dominated second spot and a weight of expectation hung around their necks.

On the pitch at Rovers there simply isn't enough evidence to have any strong opinion on him yet. Having just eight games, after the transfer window had closed, plus a suspension and injuries, was not enough to begin to judge him. Blaming Clarke for relegation is like holding Gerald Ford responsible for the Vietnam war.

Off the pitch Darrell's quest for human and financial discipline, and the pursuit of hungry non-league players, is admirable for our present state. In 2011 we temporarily had a gruff Northerner as a manager who was going to shake the club up after the gluttonous conclusion of Paul Trollope's reign. If the Board hadn't lost their bottle by sacking Dave Penney two months into the job, we probably wouldn't be where we are today. The only thing worse in life than not having any morals and discipline, is discovering some and then chucking them out of the window at the first sign of tribulation.

Even if we had still gone down under Penney that season I suspect he could still have shook the club out of its ineffective slumber off the pitch and at least laid some groundwork for a brighter future on the pitch. Dare I even offer up a prospective comparison to Ian Atkins at this point? A man often viewed as dislikeable, but a manager who stopped the rot of the early Noughties and whose squad became the backbone of the wondrous double finalists of the 2006/07 season.

'Player power' famously helped oust Martin Dobson in 1991 and also Penney two decades later, propelling them both into the record books as the two shortest lived permanent Rovers managers ever (merely 12 and 13 games respectively). I dearly hope that this dubious honour is never allowed to transpire again.

I'm not suggesting that Penney, or Clarke, are the best managers since sliced bread, but at least they are individuals who could leave a lasting legacy of human and financial discipline within the club, rather than all the other managers who left us with the futile status quo intact. After saying 'thank you very much' when offered a fat budget and minimal interference, they proceeded to bring in crocks, and hand out lardy three year contracts to 30 year old also-rans and 19 year old kids who'd had a couple of good games. This method was known as 'here's a gold plated spade, now go and dig a big hole with it', and it needlessly kept alive the unhealthy reputation Rovers had of offering big salaries with scant performance related clauses, coupled with a poor fitness and injury record, and spineless internal discipline.

I am therefore rather exasperated with unhealthy criticism of ROVERS players who most people have never even seen kick a ball. Most Gasheads asked for some younger, hungrier, attack minded players and we seem to have signed several of those, and they all appear genuinely motivated to be here. That enthusiasm should not be taken for granted. If you've ever had a job you don't really like, you'll know how harmful it can be on your performance. Many wanted a few old heads down the spine of the team, and surely we potentially have that with the 'M' team; Mildenhall, McChrystal, Mansell & Monkhouse.

I'm not a 'happy clapper'. I realise this disciplined approach may not result in an immediately competitive squad for the Conference. BUT I will try to be patient and I will let our players do their talking on the pitch, and at least when I'm asked who I support I can now look a person in the eyes and say, ok, we may be down in the dumps for the time being, but we've found a bit of backbone and aren't a pushover for washed up players or indifferent managers anymore.

Now, if only we can bring about world peace as well…

WEEK 13 – SERVANTS AND LEADERS

PUBLISHED ON THURSDAY 31ST JULY 2014

Saturday 26th July - Sixth Pre-season friendly

Gloucester City 3   Bristol Rovers 4

Chamberlain - 48', Griffin   White - 49', Parkes - 59', Sinclair - 60',
- 55', Williams - 64'   Lockyer - 73'

Rovers: Kieran Preston, Ryan Higgins, Lee Brown, Tom Lockyer, Pierce Mitchell, Tom Parkes, Romy Boco, Jake Gosling, Ryan Brunt (Matty Taylor, 46), Jamie White, Andy Monkhouse (Stuart Sinclair, 46).

Unused Substitutes: Ellis Harrison, Danny Greenslade, Dominic Thomas

Attendance: 421, inc 205 Gas

Tuesday 29th July - Extra Pre-season friendly

Cribbs FC 1   Bristol Rovers XI 1

Graffigano - 36'   Lucas - 75'

Rovers: Kent Kauppinrn, Tyler Lyttle, Danny Greenslade, Louis Ezwele, Pierce Mitchell, Jay Malpas, Ryan Broom (Donovan Wilson, 76), Dominic Thomas (George Corp, 78), Jamie Lucas, Aaron Ward-Baptiste, Tom Fry (Harrison Trueman, 57).

Servants and Leaders

When the virtually annual 'Legends' match between ex-Rovers and City players, and several blue or red minor celebs, was postponed a few months ago on May Day, I was obviously disappointed.

I had gone to the first two bouts, run by 'Kicking Out for Kids' as a fund raiser, and thoroughly enjoyed them. Let's hope it will be back next season, and won't be cancelled due to another relegation (cough!).

Vaughan Jones was scheduled to be the Rovers team captain that day. Joner is a true legend who needs no introduction to most Pirates, with over 400 appearances, and the captaincy of the record breaking 1989/90 Championship winning side.

It was intriguing to see Vaughan making a reappearance in the media last season, and I doubt I would have been alone amongst Gasheads to have hoped that the club would have invited this exceptional servant back to do an inspirational talk to our lacklustre team. Vaughan would have put a rocket up them, yet also exude the serenity he showed as the patented 'cool left back'.

Off the pitch he seemed rather modest. I was once standing in the sunshine on the Blackthorn Terrace (before the roof) wearing the old white 'Universal Components' away kit from the aforementioned Championship winning season. I got talking to a couple of blokes, as you do, and their friend behind me said in a soft treacly Welsh accent 'that's a good old top you've got on'. I turned around to be faced by Joner himself, standing on OUR terrace with his friends. My jaw almost hit the floor.

I assume that Mark McChrystal will be Captain this season. He was given the crucial role by Darrell Clarke after he removed it from Tom Parkes. As an unreconstructed centre half myself I have always rather appreciated Tom Parkes, but I felt he was only given the Captaincy as one of those classic psychological ploys to tone down the abrasive nature of his game and improve his understanding of collective responsibility on the pitch.

Tom collected nine yellow cards and a brace of reds in his 33 loan matches at other clubs before joining us. He then replicated that when he became a Pirate, with eight yellows and two reds in 34 matches before John Ward arrived. When Matt Gill and Garry Kenneth were both injured he was given the armband for the home match against Plymouth on New Year's Day 2013 and held it until Ward went upstairs.

Having the captaincy certainly mellowed that side of his game. He only received five yellows for the remaining 21 games of the 2012/13 season and as he was the League Two Player of the Month for February 2013 it certainly didn't seem to have any negative effect on his game originally.

In September 2013 Tom signed an extended and improved contract, with John Ward stating that, "He's a young man who has been made captain, and is setting an example for others. He has taken everything on board, and it has even improved his game." Eight yellows in 52 games last season, with no suspensions, certainly proved that Ward was right on part of the issue.

However, his form did decline, in approximate correlation to his waistline expanding, and the situation began to mirror that of Ward's managerial residence. Both decisions were right at the time (2012/13), but neither job tenure necessarily needed to continue into the 2013/14 season, and certainly not beyond the New Year.

Although this captaincy ploy often works with younger footballers it does rather paint the manager into a corner, as after the behavioural blemish has been cleansed they are left with the dilemma of either keeping a captain who may not actually be the best leader available to the club, or forsaking a young man who has not necessarily done anything wrong AND then having to keep him in the same team as the new captain.

Young Parksey was clearly no Joner yet. Although he tackled his card habit on the pitch he clearly wasn't a good enough example, or leader, to warrant being allowed to retain the honour of captaincy.

Some people have criticised Darrell Clarke for publicly explaining that he stripped Parkes of the captaincy because he was overweight and under fit. But what he spoke was the truth, and the truth shall set you free... eventually. Tom himself has admitted the new gaffer was right and, to his immense credit, it has motivated him to return this season so trim that some Gasheads are even wondering if it's the same man.

After reading Hermann Hesse's mystic short novel 'Journey to the East', Robert Greenleaf was inspired to formulate his ideas of servant-leadership, and wrote that "Good leaders must first become good servants".

Tom Parkes still has a decade or more ahead of him in the game and I anticipate that his new maturity as a servant will ultimately be a liberator for him.

WEEK 14 - DEAR PRUDENCE, WON'T YOU COME OUT TO PLAY

PUBLISHED ON FRIDAY 8TH AUGUST 2014

Friday 1st August - Seventh Pre-season friendly

Bristol Rovers 1   **Coventry City 2**

Taylor - 41'   Swanson - 65', Phillips - 68'

Rovers: Steve Mildenhall, Daniel Leadbitter, Tom Parkes, Tom Lockyer (Pierce Mitchell), Mark McChrystal (Lee Mansell), Lee Brown, Andy Monkhouse (Jamie White), Ollie Clarke (Jake Gosling), Stuart Sinclair, Matty Taylor, Ryan Brunt (Ellis Harrison).

Unused Substitute: Kieran Preston

Attendance: 1,821, inc 120 Lady Godiva's

Dear Prudence, won't you come out to play

At both the recent Supporters Club EGM, and the Fan's Forum Q&A, we were consistently reminded how our club apparently wouldn't exist without additional funding from some of our Board of Directors.

We were also rather curiously given a new scapegoat to flog for past financial imprudence; Lennie Lawrence, our Director of Football in the mid to late 2000's. I must have missed his obituary in the newspaper as the frankly rambling accusations levelled against him smacked more of kicking a dead corpse than a humble acceptance that the Board and Senior Staff simply didn't set professional budgets or adequately monitor the outcomes of these large spends.

We are now also being told that they need 9,500 people through the turnstiles in order to balance the books, and as the reality is around 6,500 and set to fall, that the shortfall has been regularly covered by our dear leader in the sky, and a few of his associates.

Not only is that financial analysis extremely simplistic in itself (what about player sales, increased revenue by running the club better, etc?) but more importantly is this really the benchmark we judge a well run club by? Are they suggesting that if we had crowds of 9,500 then everything would be hunky dory, and we could then positively afford to waste money on sick notes and lardy three year contracts?

I'm not an accountant, but I can read a set of accounts and I can smell financial imprudence from a mile away. Considering how badly we've done when making a massive loss each year I'd suggest we can't do much worse by trying to be financially prudent.

Don't get me wrong, I do appreciate that they try, and that recently several small initiatives at the club suggest they have taken on board several of the frustrations us average fans have. But, I want them to sort out this budget once and for all.

I don't want the Board to set a budget that is impossible to be balanced, and then constantly dip their hands in their pockets as a matter of uncontrolled routine.

I don't want the Board to then tell us there wouldn't be a club without them. This perpetual position of failure is nothing to be proud of; it's merely a self fulfilling prophesy if they continue to run the club the way they always have done! A Machiavellian cynic could even argue that it is a state of domination that is actively encouraged as a method of princely control over the plebeian fans like you and I. 'Shut up, be happy' as the rabble rousers Jello Biafra and Ice-T derided.

I don't want players to be sold and then little of the money re-invested in the team, under the pretext that the losses have been so big in our imprudent playing budget that the player profit needs to go into the pot labelled 'gaping losses'.

I don't want the board to give a Gallic shrug of the shoulders when reminded that we get crowds of 6,500, not 9,500, and will suffer more each time we drop a division.

I don't want the Board to suggest that there is nothing they can do about this financial Armageddon, even though it happens EVERY season, with EVERY manager. The reason Einstein's quote that "The definition of insanity is doing the same thing over and over again and expecting different results" is so over used in the media is precisely because it is so apposite.

I want them to take control of this situation, like they would in any other challenge in life, and to budget for Prudence to be asked to come out to play.

I want the board to budget for 6,500 fans (or whatever is now realistic given less away fans...) and then set a playing budget to reflect that. AND stick to it, yet remain flexible if more investment would really make a difference.

Then when the Board need to put their hands in their pockets it will be to fund something exceptional, such as a player who will make a real difference to the squad, some training or physio equipment that will improve us, or even capital spending on the training ground, team facilities, etc.

Under this system any 'windfalls' from player sales, previous sell-on/add-on clauses, cup runs, and TV coverage, should primarily be invested into the playing budget. It's a style rather like the performance related clauses that I have always championed in player contracts. The better you do the more financial reward you get to push onwards.

Thankfully they have, by accident, realised that yet another relegation (our third now whilst at the Mem), the loss of the rugby club, and the legal delays affecting the UWE stadium, has created the perfect storm, and this triumvirate of misery will make a MASSIVE difference to our income. Reduced TV money, no Football League money, no rugby money, various planning and legal costs, less away fans. Not even the yearly First Round defeat to a Championship side in the League Cup, or the chance of a decent run in the Football League Trophy. The list is almost endless. Therefore something HAS to be done now and Darrell Clarke is now 'on the case' when recruiting affordable players.

Meanwhile, on the pitch the cabin fever is over and we get to watch REAL football this weekend. Not friendlies where people with probably too much time on their hands try to scrutinise the inscrutable, but REAL football, with three points at stake.

I can small gas, and I can't wait to cheer the lads on again. Even if we can't be proud of the way the club has been run, we have many authentic, sincere fans that we can be proud of.

WEEK 15 – LITTLE AND LARGE

PUBLISHED ON FRIDAY 15TH AUGUST 2014

Saturday 9th August - Conference

Bristol Rovers 0   **Grimsby Town 0**

Rovers: Mildenhall, Leadbitter [Booked] (Gosling – 66'), Parkes, McChrystal (Capt.), Lockyer, Brown, Sinclair, Mansell, Monkhouse (Clarke – 73'), Brunt (White – 79'), Taylor.

Unused Substitutes: Preston, Harrison.

Attendance: 7,019, inc 452 Fishmen   Referee: Simon Bennett

Tuesday 12th August - Conference

Barnet 2   **Bristol Rovers 0**

Akinde - 22', MacDonald - 43'

Rovers: Puddy, Lockyer (Leadbitter - 53'), McChrystal (Capt.), Trotman (Parkes - 46'), Brown, Gosling (Brunt - 65'), Sinclair, Monkhouse, Mansell, Taylor, White

Unused Substitutes: Ollie Clarke, Harrison

Attendance: 2,027, inc 663 Gas   Referee: Rob Whitton

Little and Large

Against all the odds (August holidays, live on TV, and being in the, cough, fifth tier) it was great to see a 7,000 crowd at the Mem on Saturday. That was higher than every match in League Two, five matches in League One, and also within a busload of Swindon Town. And fair play to the Mariners for having 452 in the away end, something we may rarely see this season.

We seem to be a bit of a 'Little and Large' team at the moment. I thought the little 'uns (Taylor, Sinclair, Gosling, Mansell, and the cameo we saw from Jamie White) showed some promise, but the big 'uns were a bit laboured. One tall player, who I don't really wish to single out, was hopefully sorely off colour because he showed none of the high tempo that Clarke says he demands.

Reports from Barnet suggest that little has been learnt yet from numerous previous seasons, where our little un's got poor service from the large boys who either don't seem to fully understand the game plan, or are not capable of executing it. I am prepared to give them time though.

The rest of the results on Saturday were interesting, nay worrying, as it seemed like all the 'large' clubs comfortably beat the 'little' clubs, and that the Rovers match was rather exceptional, being goalless and between two well known ex-league teams.

During Rovers' best spell, in the second half rain (which incidentally made me wonder if we should water the pitch before kick off as most higher level teams do), the obligatory 'guy behind me on the terrace' chose a strange time to say, "well, this isn't in the script", as if looking a decent passing side at times and drawing to last season's fourth best team is some sort of disgrace. Us Gasheads have been incredibly patient in the long run given 15 years of mainly failure, but our short term patience is often non-existent, and calls for Darrell Clarke's head already make me uneasy about the impetuosity some of us have coursing through our red blooded veins. Not that long ago they didn't even bother making League tables for the first three games of the season. Of course the points are just as important as a crucial win in late April, but to panic too much about a position in a 'table' on the 13th of August could be construed as losing your nerve.

I was also at Wolves vs. Norwich on Sunday as my best friend is a Canary. I turned to him before kick off and relayed a stat I'd read on a web site, that Norwich hadn't won their opening game of the season for 12 years. The last time they did win was in 2002 in the Championship, against, yes, you guessed it, Grimsby Town.

I'm not suggesting that Grimsby's proud history means we shouldn't beat them, but we need to put the result into perspective. Not losing your first home match is important and something we have regularly failed to achieve in recent years; Paul Buckle's first home game in 2011 against his ex-employer, amidst banners in the away end proclaiming him a 'Judas', had 'revenge' written all over it, and the tame loss to Oxford United in 2012 was the first of many nails in Mark McGhee's coffin.

There have been two inescapable concerns though that seem to have followed us over from League Two. One is the lack of goals; zero for us, whereas 12 of the 24 teams in the division have already scored three goals or more. The other is a consistent team. Our 1989/90 Third Tier championship team included four players who started all of the 46 League games, and there were four others with over 40 starts. In contrast we already have four of our starting line-up from Saturday who can't be ever presents.

Given that we faced another solid ex-league team on Tuesday, I feel that the first real test will be this Saturday, against Altrincham, a team who've lost both matches and have only just emerged from three seasons in the Conference North.

The two games so far have not been the shock of the new that we probably needed. In fact it's almost as though the Conference planners wanted to ease us into the division, with games against teams we have regularly played in the past, on crisp lush grass, and in stadiums that at least have a vague air of League football circling around them.

Eddie and Syd may even be with us in spirit on Saturday. Rovers fans drank in Syd's pub in Fleetwood last season, and Eddie lives in Portishead and despite being a huge Man City fan has been to the Rovers before. If anyone can make a mediocre 'Little and Large' combination work, they surely can!

QI STATS - FISHY FACTS

The Conference season started with Rovers vs. Grimsby Town, contesting an early kick-off on 9th August 2014, and finished with us playing each other in the Play-Off Final for another draw on 19th May 2015.

Lenell John-Lewis scored for the Mariners at Wembley on his 26th birthday. It was his last game for Grimsby before his transfer to Newport County, where he is never knowingly under played.

WEEK 16 - WHERE HAVE ALL THE HEROES GONE?

PUBLISHED ON THURSDAY 21ST AUGUST 2014

Saturday 16th August - Conference

Altrincham 2 **Bristol Rovers 1**

Reeves - 18', McChrystal (og) - 65' Mansell - 76'

Rovers: Mildenhall, Leadbitter (Gosling - 59'), Parkes [Booked], McChrystal (Capt.), Brown, Sinclair [Dismissed], Mansell, Clarke (White - 74"), Martin, Brunt [Booked] (Monkhouse - 68'), Taylor [Booked].

Unused Substitutes: Puddy, Trotman

Attendance: 1,463, inc 376 Gas   Referee: Ross Joyce

Played 3 Points 1 Position   *Gap to leaders [FC Halifax Town] = 8 points*
19th

Where have all the heroes gone?

At the inaugural meeting of the Bristol Rovers Independent Supporters Association (BRISA) a few weeks ago one of the more light hearted comments was how the most 'positive' thing that has happened to this club in the last six months was to sign a bloke with a massive beard and a bush of straggly hair.

And he was right, despite the harebrained red card he got at the weekend.

Gasheads have taken Stuart Sinclair to their hearts immediately... well, immediately after the jokes about looking like a tramp, a fisherman, or even Worzel Gummidge, had subsided.

Sinclair (hereafter to be referred to as 'The Beard') was cleverly used to advertise the Grimsby match. The headline 'the fight back begins' also seemed to have a punchy humility that many fans sought from the club and off the pitch it looks as if there are several small sprouts of professionalism growing at our club. On the pitch is another story of course, but the pain of being defeated by part-timers may be precisely the tough love that can rouse some of our players from their slumber. Quite why professional footballers need a 'wake up call' to smell the non-league coffee is beyond me, but then again we are the fans who apparently had to lower our expectations in 2011. Three long years later and I fail to see how they can get any lower. At least it is better to learn now than later and maybe our difficult first five fixtures are what we need. What took Luton four seasons to learn, we can hopefully learn in a few challenging months.

'The Beard' became a cult hero at Rovers before he'd even kicked a ball in anger. He was rightly named MOTM vs. Grimsby and during the match I heard several shouts (including mine) of 'Great tackle the Beard'. 'Sinclair's Beard' even has its own [fake] twitter account.

So where have the cult heroes gone? Is it just me, or does the game have so few of them now? The late 80s and early 90s was full of them.

'**Ollie** is probably unique in recent years as both a cult hero and an absolute hero. Over 450 appearances in three different spells, plus 4½ seasons as manager. His ferret like performances, being an unflappable penalty taker, and for sporting awful shades and a curly perm on the open top bus around Kingswood in May 1990, whilst shouting things about City through a flimsy megaphone.

We had **Brian Parkin** for showing us his bottom all the time, **Devon 'Bruno' White** for his knack of scoring important goals, **Carl Saunders** for asking a local reporter why the adoring fans called him 'Billy Ocean' all the time, and **Ian Alexander** for scaring the bejabers out of attackers, particularly City wingers, and randomly taking his false teeth out to emphasize his psychosis. Jocky was actually well ahead of his time though, as a winger who was converted into a right back. These days full backs are routinely expected to do those two roles most games. Jocky had three roles actually, as when Mr.Glum was sent off against Brighton in March 1991 it was Jocky who went in goal, and immediately saved the resulting penalty from John Byrne. That really is the stuff of legend, although **Bob Bloomer**, the classic utility man, deserves a special mention for also going in goal when Parkin was injured in an FA Cup match that same season. Since the 1993/94 season, when three subs were allowed, we have sadly rarely seen the hilarious sight of an outfield player hurriedly pulling on a padded jersey three sizes too big for him.

Dennis Bailey is another, and he was only a loanee. He plundered 10 goals in 19 games in 1989, including a legendary goal at Molineux to dispatch Wolves to their only home defeat for the entire season, but unfortunately was not allowed to appear in the Play-Off final against Port Vale. He returned for a cameo loan spell in 1991 (1 goal in 6 games) and then became most famous for his sublime televised hat trick for QPR against a shell shocked Man United on New Years Day 1992. It was masterminded by Gerry Francis, included 'Ollie in midfield, and is still the last league hat trick to ever be scored at Old Trafford by an away team.

Nearly every player had a nickname in those days. These days the turnover of players is often so rapid it's more likely they will have 'Who?' on the back of their shirt than Smash, Grab, Punky, Scooter, The Beast, The Duke, or Gravy.

Cult heroes of the 2000's surely include:

Steve Elliott for being flaming brilliant, and loving Rovers like rarely seen before or since. Drinking (in moderation of course...) in the local pubs and being a decent guy.

Sir Rickie of Lambert for bucket loads of goals and assists, but particularly that goal vs. City to take us to the final of the Johnstone's Paint Trophy in 2007. Basso prayed to his God but the shot had already rocketed past him.

Little **Sammy Igoe** for the keystone cops goal in the last minute of the Play-Off Final later that season. After Shrewsbury's keeper went up for late corner, the ball broke to Igoe, 5 foot nothing, and utterly shattered. He ran and ran until he could run no more, and with leaden legs he finally hit a weak shot towards the empty net as the breath of his pursuers could be felt on his neck. It seemed to take an age to get to the line and as it trickled over a Shrews defender slid into the back of the net to vainly try to rescue it, whilst 40,000 Gasheads went wild.

Some cult heroes have had mere fleeting moments in a Gas shirt but they have been so crucial that they'll never need to pay for a drink again in our beautiful city. In Uncle Ray Graydon's first season, in 2002/03, Rovers were constantly in the bottom five from early November onwards and were only 'rescued' by the most dramatic Easter resurrection since a certain fellow two Millennia previously. **Andy Rammell** may have only played seven games for us and scored only in those three crucial wins, but we would have been goners without even half of those 10 points from the last four games of the season.

Is it possible for flops to be cult heroes, in a derisive way? If so, the list is almost endless, especially during the current Millennium. After disregarding Mickey Evans, Paul Tait ('he's a goal machine' was surely a sick joke?), Robbie

Ryan, Justin Richards and Rob Quinn for being slightly too, cough, good, I offer you **Moussa Dagnogo**, with two sub appearances in 2000 and so out of his depth that we wondered whether he was the famous Ali Dia in disguise, and **Michel Kuipers**, an ex-Dutch marine, who with Lee Jones injured in March 1999, got just a solitary start for us losing at Bournemouth. When Jones was injured again 'Ollie had so much confidence in him that he rapidly recruited Antony Williams to play eight games, and in the 'dead rubber' last game of the season the gloves were given instead to a YTS lad Ray Johnston, his only ever start... EVER! The next season was barely better as adolescent loanees Stuart Taylor and Rhys Evans were given the nod before him and even dear old Brian Parkin was roped back in for his first games for four years. Kuipers played 280 games for Brighton after us so he is a genuine cult hero at the Seagulls, rather than the cult zero he is with us.

Now is the time for the new crop of heroes to step forward. Come on the Beard. Come on the Gas!

WEEK 17 - A LINE IN THE SAND

PUBLISHED ON FRIDAY 29TH AUGUST 2014

Saturday 23rd August - Conference

Bristol Rovers 1   **AFC Telford United 0**

Ollie Clarke - 55'

Rovers: Mildenhall, Lockyer, Parkes, Trotman, Brown, Monkhouse, Mansell (Capt.), Clarke [Booked],, Martin [Booked],, Cunnington, Taylor (Harrison - 87').

Unused Substitutes: Puddy, Leadbitter, Gosling, White.

Attendance: 5,450, inc 167 Bucks   Referee: Mark Pottage

Bank Holiday Monday 25th August - Conference

Forest Green Rovers 1   **Bristol Rovers 1**

Parkin - 68'   Monkhouse - 55'

Rovers: Mildenhall, Lockyer [Booked], Parkes, Trotman [Booked], Brown, Monkhouse, Mansell (Capt.), Clarke, Martin (Sinclair - 78'), Cunnington (Harrison - 49'), Taylor (White - 84').

Unused Substitutes: Puddy, Gosling.

Attendance: 3,781, inc 1,886 Gas   Referee: Steven Rushton

Played 5 Points 5 Position 16th   *Gap to leaders [FC Halifax Town] = 10 points*

A Line in The Sand

Last week I was asked why I included a large dollop of nostalgia in my blog. Shouldn't I be banging on every week about the state we are in, on and off the pitch?

This column has no remit, except to write about Bristol Rovers F.C.. I have no axe to grind, and no baggage of being involved with Rovers or any Supporters groups at any level, ever.

I'm not a sports reporter so I won't be kicking every ball for the readers after each match, I'm not a politician so I won't be following every step up the greasy pole that Charlotte Leslie takes, and I'm not a businessman so I won't be unduly caught up in which moneyed man (it is always a man) has bought his way onto the Board of Directors so he can take decisions that us fans should rightfully be taking ourselves. A fundamental problem with football in our country is that it is built on a completely cock-eyed model of capitalist ownership, but that's probably a blog for another day.

I am an experienced terrace fan who likes to write, and likes to analyse. Many of my articles so far have been very critical of the Board of Directors, but I'm not going to solely concentrate on them every week. Many of my articles have been very supportive of Darrell Clarke, or more accurately the principles on which he is trying to run the footballing side of our club, but I won't be an apologist for him every week either.

When your club is this pitiable you need nostalgia to keep you sane. I went on a tangent because I refused to be drawn into the negative, and often very bitter and divisive, Internet meltdown after just three games. The season lasts more than eight months, not eight days.

Nine days later I also refuse to be waving a promotion flag, despite four handy points in two games, and vastly improved performances.

Life is far more nuanced than the black and white thinking that the loudest voices seem to espouse. We are a team in development; a complex work in progress. Howard Hodgkin, now a world renowned abstract painter, used to teach art and printmaking in my local town, Corsham. As his method matured, his mode was to work on a new canvas, then turn it around out of sight for several years of reflection before returning to it, to reassess and build on his principles some more. That of course is at the extreme end of the patient and pensive scale, but surely us Gasheads could learn a little patience now that we finally have a manager who is working hard within a budget rather than giving stupid contracts to the likes of Garry Kenneth and Matt Gill, or stalking players like James Constable and John-Joe O'Toole who clearly didn't want to be at our valiant club.

On Monday we were treated to the laughingly entitled 'Gloucestershire Derby'. Rovers dominated the game and looked quite good, despite the disappointing result. I wish we'd beaten Forest Green Rovers though, if only to bestow karmic payback for fielding probably the most dis-likeable XI ever seen on a pitch.

As much as I find the eco and ethical philosophy of their club off the pitch extremely constructive, it seems completely disingenuous if the manager is then permitted to employ Lee Hughes (a killer sentenced to six years in prison, and later convicted of a separate assault), David Pipe (sentenced to three years two months for GBH), and Danny Coles, an infant trapped in an adults body.

To see these players at a progressive club like FGR is akin to a bad dream in which Gandhi owns shares in an arms manufacturer and Linda McCartney and Franz Kafka are 'round the back of the bike sheds munching on bacon butties. I know which side of the line I stand on.

One weakness I've noticed in non-league footy is that many players have a poor first touch, often having their first, second and third touches all in one heavy prod. This disease will not be helping goal scorers, including our own. Three goals in five games; and none by a recognised striker. Although Matty Taylor has shown real signs of sprightly exuberance up front, there are two ways to look at the number of clear chances he has failed to convert. You can either see these chances as positive, as he is in the right place at the right time and one day some of them may go in, or you could more simply conclude that he isn't much of a goal scorer at this point in his development.

Which makes me reflect on the $64,000 question, or more likely the £200,000 question.

It is quite remarkable that most of the best strikers in our recent history have all cost us about the same. Rickie Lambert, Nathan Ellington, Jason Roberts, Barry Hayles, Jamie Cureton and Junior Agogo (part swap deal), all came in at between £150,000 and £250,000, as if there was an Einsteinian formula where the answer was pretty much constant.

I realise it seems like a lot of money, but a proven goal scorer is one of the few positions on the pitch where their contribution really can be quantified, and not only that, it can also be very profitable, with just the sales of the first four players mentioned above raking in a profit of over £6m.

Of course there have been some relatively expensive flops as well, such as Mickey Evans, Justin Richards, Darryl Duffy and Andy Williams, but that shouldn't put us off wisely spending some money just on this one all important position.

BRISTOL ROVERS FAN'S VIEW

BRFC 2 - FC HALIFAX TOWN 1

PUBLISHED ON MONDAY 1ST SEPTEMBER 2014

FC Halifax Town, the phoenix club from the flames, got well and truly burnt.

How many times is it us Rovers fans who have rued missed chances whilst the other side always seem to score soft or scrappy goals?

The boot was on the other foot on Saturday, with Rovers (mainly) withstanding constant second half pressure before Ellis Harrison popped up to score a goal he knew little about, via a sweet cross from Stuart Sinclair, who has more of a turn of pace than his beard may suggest.

It was an entertaining game... when the ball was on the floor. On the 15 minute mark an air raid siren sounded as Halifax got their first throw-in in our half, and unleashed their long spinning throw-in specialist. Two minutes later we witnessed their first long keeper kick right up to our 18 yard box. Both tactics were rather superfluous as they were a very handy team on the floor.

The first half gave us a glimpse of what Rovers can achieve, with Dave Martin showing wing skills we haven't seen for a while, and Jamie White chasing an almost lost cause to hook in the cross for Adam Cunnington's archetypal centre forward header.

Steve Mildenhall may not be the best in the air, as witnessed in the lead up to Forest Green Rovers' goal last Monday, but he is one of the best shot stoppers around, and preserved our lead with a strong hand to a vicious free kick from just outside the 18 yard box, and barely a minute later won a one on one clash on the 6 yard line with the ever dangerous Scott Boden.

Meanwhile referee Brett Huxtable gave a comedic performance more akin to Cliff Huxtable from 'The Cosby Show' and Tom Lockyer struggled out of position at right back, even though a right back (Leadbitter) sat on the bench.

To their credit Halifax always sought to attack, unlike other teams, and for a large part of the second half us Blackthorn terracers hardly saw the ball without the aid of binoculars.

But as they say 'you have to be in it to win it', and by standing firm at 1-1 we always gave ourselves a chance of mugging a win.

I WAS ASKED TO WRITE THE BRISTOL ROVERS FAN'S VIEW IN THE BRISTOL POST - THIS WAS IT...

WEEK 18 – TASTE THE DIFFERENCE

PUBLISHED ON FRIDAY 5TH SEPTEMBER 2014

Saturday 30th August - Conference

Bristol Rovers 2   **FC Halifax Town 1**

Cunnington - 27', Harrison - 90'   Boden - 62'

Rovers: Mildenhall, Lockyer [Booked], Parkes, Trotman, Brown, Monkhouse [Booked], Clarke, Mansell (Capt.), Martin (Sinclair – 66'), White (Harrison – 60'), Cunnington.

Unused Substitutes: Puddy, Leadbitter, Brunt.

Attendance: 5,394, inc 260 Shaymen   Referee: Brett Huxtable

Played 6 Points 8 Position 15th *Gap to leaders [Barnet] = 7 points*

Taste the Difference

The Bristol Rovers Supporters Club is currently electing a so-called fan's director to join the BRFC Board of Directors. If this role had any real power it could be dangerous. As it is the fan's directors forage on crumbs from the biscuit platter of affluent businessmen and are mere flies on the Boardroom wall. One of the current incumbents, the apparently affable Brian Seymour-Smith, rather implausibly has the audacity to be standing for re-election despite being party to all the decisions taken over the last three years that have led to non-league football and the worst board / fan relationship ever seen. This is the man who labelled dissenters 'keyboard warriors', and had the temerity to tell fans to "pull together" at the end of last season, as if 4,300 Gasheads at the last two away games, and 18,000 at the last two home games, wasn't already 'pulling together'. If either him or Ken Masters had any dignity they would have stepped away from the board in May, and admit they can't simultaneously claim to be equal members of the top table, but not equally responsible for the fine mess we are in.

Personally I have voted for Rod Chapman in a vain hope to elect someone who might stand up to the Board; however, as the Board ludicrously reserve the right to veto any electee, it would actually be a badge of honour if they didn't think the winner was acceptable to them.

In a scene reminiscent of the film adaptation of 'Brewster's Millions' many members may metaphorically vote 'None of the Above' as they wonder if anyone can really shake that Boardroom out of its conceited malaise? How important this position is does rather depend on what you want a fan's director to do. If you want them to help get new TVs in the clubroom, rather than stand up for the fan's on crucial Boardroom votes, then of course this position is suddenly important to your comfy little middle of the road existence. Personally I want a lot more from my so-called rep than that; I want a fighter, not a suit.

Meanwhile the news that Sainsbury's don't seem to want to complete the agreement to buy the Mem has not been a total surprise.

Like a game of Cluedo, there were small scraps of information that never quite added up. Sainsbury's were not represented at the Judicial Review even though they were the 'First Interested Party'. There was the general climate of supermarkets issuing profit warnings and proclaiming that times were tough (it was Tesco last week), and the specific example of Sainsbury's pulling out of large developments elsewhere and being prepared to write-off £92m of up-front costs. Fans were twitching because even basic ground-work had failed to start even though to the man in the street there didn't seem to be any more serious impediments to overcome. And finally I really started to worry when all four local MP's were writing an open letter to Sainsbury's asking them to make their position clear. Something like that doesn't come about without a prod from people with gigantic vested inter-ests in the development, & seemingly a poker face that was slowly withering.

Throughout all of this there was either a wall of silence from the Board when fans and the press asked 'difficult' questions, or a stock answer about 'confidentiality'. Nick Higgs persistently squirmed when faced with contin-ued questions about when the stadium build will start, and more recently if the contract with Sainsbury's really was tighter than a gnat's bottom. During all of this I was waiting for a reporter to turn to him, do a hammy Kenneth Williams impression and say 'ooooh, the lady doth protest too much, me-thinks'. As far as I could see, with NO inside info nor being a friend of that bloke down the pub who knows the milkman of the youth coach, it has been looking like a battle of compensation for quite a while now, with the culprit being Mr Recession with the cheap cucumber in the produce aisle, rather than Professor Plum with the iron pipe in the library.

I doubt Nick Higgs will ever make a decent poker player, which also presumably explains his bizarre ramblings at the Fans Q&A about how Lennie Lawrence would allegedly get the Board to pay more than they initially thought they were paying a player. They must have all spotted the 'tells' of a man who had just sold his business for millions and didn't know much about the inside dealings of football or contract law. Dare I even drag up the old idiom that a fool and his money are soon parted?

Of course I have sympathy for our great leader in the sky, and still have respect for his efforts. I am NOT labelling him a fool, but this is starting to look like one of the biggest follies in our history, as whilst the eye was taken off the football on the pitch we got relegated to non-league. The Mem may not be a good stadium but at least it is 'our' stadium and will remain so, whereas there is no guarantee that we will ever even return to League football. What is truly worrying is how long this has been going on for 'behind the scenes'. The court writ gives details of issues going back to July 2013. I would suggest the Board hardly had any time at all for the playing side of the club, as if writing off the entire season as a poor one on the pitch, without any thought of a relegation battle. Toni Watola's infamous comment that they hadn't budgeted for Rovers being relegated because we were only in the relegation zone for 70 minutes all season will live very long in our memories (he was surprisingly inaccurate for a Director of Finance as well, as it was in fact only 54 minutes).

The real quirk of fate is that the red half of the City have the money but not the permission, and we have the permission but not the money. None of these tedious legal issues would have even been needed if we had £30m, and work could have started back in July 2012 when planning permission for the UWE Stadium was granted by a benign South Gloucestershire Council. As Hargreaves Lansdown continue to post amazing results, that figure is quite literally pocket money to Steve Lansdown.

WEEK 19 - THE 36 STEPS

PUBLISHED ON WEDNESDAY 10TH SEPTEMBER 2014

Saturday 6th September - Conference

Braintree Town 2   Bristol Rovers 0

Davis (Pen) - 31', Sparkes - 59'

Rovers: Mildenhall, Lockyer, Parkes [Booked] (Sinclair - 63'), Trotman, Brown, Monkhouse, Mansell [Booked] (Capt.), Clarke, Martin, White (Taylor - 60'), Cunnington (Brunt - 74')

Unused Substitutes: Puddy, Donovan Wilson.

Attendance: 1,621, inc 565 Gas   Referee: Daniel Cook

Played 7 Points 8 Position 15th   *Gap to leaders [Barnet] = 10 points*

The 36 Steps

There are many reasons why a team fails to achieve over a long season. One can be a threadbare squad. Another is away form.

Unlike League football the Conference schedules a lot of midweek games for the first half of the season. This is really going to test our thin squad NOW. We play mid week fixtures in four out of the next five weeks. That's 10 games in 36 days. The all action hero Richard Hannay may have had his 39 Steps, but we've got 36 to face in order to make a serious impact here.

Overall there are seven mid week games scheduled between this week and Christmas. With the traditionally hectic festive period to follow, there is no let up until 2015. For you statto fans out there, a rather bizarre fact is that we will have played both Barnet and Wrexham home and away by the start of December, with all four games being Tuesday night games!

I appreciate that if (massive if...) we were in the League and had good runs in the League Cup and the Johnstone's Paint Trophy (JPT), then our schedule could be similar, but let's be realistic. In the last six seasons of our league status we only got past the first round of the League Cup or the JPT three times out of 12 attempts. Four out of six FA Cup endeavours were fallers at the first fence as well. Overall, our average number of cup games played was less than five per season.

Our squad has therefore never been tested like it will be now, yet we have only 18 players who could genuinely be considered first team players or trusted subs. It's certainly a strange time for the official BRFC fan blog to be concluding that our squad is "well equipped". Yes, about as well equipped as Jefferson Louis was to lead our forward line in 2005.

Our subs bench on Saturday included 17 year old bench debutant Donovan Wilson. I am conscious that three players were away on International duty (I hope I don't get to use that phrase often...) but if that is the best we can do in early September, it is rather worrying for the rest of a very long season.

Hopefully Darrell Clarke and the club have a plan for this and all the other niggles that are affecting us. A right back, Daniel Leadbitter, has been sitting on the bench but it seems clear that DC doesn't want to play him, even when Tom Lockyer had a torrid time against FC Halifax Town's exciting winger Jamie Jackson and needed protecting from his own efforts to get himself sent off. Jake Gosling had a promising cameo at the opening game of the season but hasn't featured since, Jamie White isn't 100% match fit by the look of him, and Ryan Brunt continues to just make us all scratch our heads and wonder whether he will ever be the special player we caught a glimpse of when he first came to the club.

Thankfully discipline (and therefore possible suspensions) is good so far. We don't have a hot headed John Joe O'Toole to cope with, and as analysed in a previous blog, Tom Parkes is no longer the card machine he used to be. We also have very few injuries at the moment, but it is a punishing schedule ahead.

We are therefore just about getting away with it at the moment, but there is a lot in our squad that is not ideal, including having two loan players who are pretty much guaranteed a place in the starting XI, and a brace of players on short term contracts (Trotman and Puddy). Having four important players who are not guaranteed to be there in a few months time is not ideal for medium-term squad development.

The good news is that there are no scheduled mid week games after New Year. The bad news is that this is merely to allow for rescheduled matches and a potentially protracted FA Trophy run. The FA Trophy requires seven games to appear in the Final, with the later round games bunched into about

30 days between late January and late February. Fans of other Conference dwellers have already warned us that although going to Wembley is nice, getting out of the League is far more important and the Trophy can be a real distraction.

Last season Cambridge United won it, and played eight games overall. Later in the season they also had three play-off games. With three FA Cup matches thrown in for good measure, they played 60 games in a season. They did it successfully though, so at least that proves it is possible... if your squad can cope.

After yet another weak away defeat, where 565 loyal Gasheads deserved far far better for their efforts, you really do have to wonder if there is something wrong with our preparation for away fixtures, or more simply something amiss with our psychology of playing away from home. Last season we had the worst away record in the league, with just 14 points taken from a possible 69 on offer. We also failed to score in 43% of matches and had the lowest scoring attack in the league.

This is a problem that has been going on for longer than just a sickening relegation season though. Previous seasons were not massively better. Even going back to the 2009/10 season, a seemingly benign mid-table finish in League One hid a poor tally of 20 points on the road. 2010/11 brought 20 again, 2011/12 gave us 21, and 2012/13 saw a positively nosebleed inducing 23 points. All in all this adds up to a pathetic 99 away points out of the last 119 away games, with a staggering goal difference of minus 80 goals.

Decent home form will usually keep you in with a vague chance of the play-offs, but atrocious away form will scupper that. And a word of warning to those happy to write off away performances as long as you keep the home crowds happy. Gillingham got relegated from League One in the 2009/10 season despite earning 44 points at the Priestfield Stadium. A derisory six away points saw them go down on goal difference.

WEEK 20 - WE ARE ALL EQUAL...

PUBLISHED ON THURSDAY 18TH SEPTEMBER 2014

Tuesday 9th September - Conference

Bristol Rovers 1   Wrexham 0

Monkhouse - 34'

Rovers: Mildenhall, Lockyer, Parkes, Trotman, Brown, Mansell (Capt.), Sinclair, Martin (Gosling - 84'), Monkhouse, Taylor, Cunnington.

Unused Substitutes: Puddy, Clarke, White, Balanta.

Attendance: 5,082, inc 230 Dragons   Referee: Lee Swabey

Saturday 13th September - Conference

Lincoln City 2   Bristol Rovers 3

Newton (Pen) - 37', Burrow - 45'   Sinclair - 13', Leadbitter - 22', Harrison - 90'

Rovers: Mildenhall, Leadbitter (Martin - 62' [Booked]), Lockyer, Parkes, Trotman, Brown, Sinclair, Clarke, Mansell (Capt.), Monkhouse (Harrison - 53'), Taylor (Cunnington - 71').

Unused Substitutes: Puddy, McChrystal.

Attendance: 2,933, inc 211 Gas   Referee: Ben Toner

Played 9 Points 14 Position 12th   *Gap to leaders [Barnet] = 8 points*

We are all equal...

As I have consistently affirmed, I really like Darrell Clarke and what he is trying to do at Rovers, although I suppose more accurately I should articulate that what I really like are the PRINCIPLES on which he is trying to lead this team, even if the practise is proving hard at the moment. I believe the way we are going now is quite literally the only avenue we have left, e.g. younger hungrier players, an attacking mind set, shorter contracts, performance related pay / incentives, a smattering of short term 'try before you buy' contracts, mainly getting players who have been good at conference level rather than other options and they have failed. I don't want a return to long contracts, old school managers, big names, declining players, inflated wages, and agents fees. Of course the problem has been to find such players and then to see if he can make it all work together. So far he's done ok, but last week we were possibly just hours away from seeing a disgraceful change of managers, only eight games into the season!

Darrell has a very tall task, but I feel we really have to stick with it, especially in this first season. We wouldn't let Dave Penney re-arrange our comfy sofas when we needed it and I hope that doesn't happen again. I can't see any point in yet another manager, especially one who could reverse the principles that we are currently striving to live by.

Am I totally happy with it all so far? No, there are some annoying itches of course. The tinkering, the lack of goals, and I can hardly believe I am writing the following line but I think we may have a football manager who actually talks too much. We probably shouldn't be told some of the things that are on his mind, particularly about player performance, and maybe some of the detail about his attempts to strengthen the squad should also be kept behind closed doors. I don't think I need to hear again how so-and-so didn't want to come to Rovers, or fit into our reduced budget.

Regularly talking about 'ex-league' clubs also seems to suggest we still haven't totally got the reality that all teams are equal in the Conference Premier. The fact that a team is an ex-league team should mean nothing when facing them. Absolutely nothing. As an example, Altrincham were formed in 1891, 35 years before the original incarnation of Aldershot, and won the Conference twice in the early 1980's when clubs weren't guaranteed entry to the Football League, so why do some still treat an ex-league team like Aldershot differently, as if there are extra points at stake when we play them? It almost seems like Orwell's allegorical line in Animal Farm, that "All animals are equal; but some animals are more equal than others", is believed by some of us.

We still need to stop feeling sorry for ourselves and I'd love to see even more of us getting behind our manager and team. We still talk about 1883, 84 years of League membership, beating the Busby Babes, winning the Watney Cup and being the first bottom tier team to beat a Premiership team in the FA Cup, almost as if we are unique. We aren't unique. In fact to a dispassionate outsider we are positively 'middle of the road' in many respects. We aren't the only old League club to fall like this so let's stop pretending we are and let's fight back. There are actually five clubs (or their direct predecessors) older than us in the Conference Premier, and two (Grimsby Town and Lincoln City) who have lost even longer periods of League membership than us. Nine Conference Premier teams have had more than 50 seasons each in the Football League. Grimsby Town spent 10 seasons out of 11 in the Championship between 1992 and 2003, yet three relegations in eight years and they were in the Conference! Imagine how their fans feel.

Dare I even mention Stockport County, currently in the Sixth Tier, who had 106 consecutive years in the Football League and were in the Third Tier as recently as 2009/10. Torquay United and Wrexham (formed in 1864; the third oldest professional club in Britain) have also been in the third Tier of the League within the last 10 years, and even Macclesfield Town had a sole season there in 1998/99. Can I stop now please?

Probably my biggest bug bear though is forgetting that nearly all the Conference teams, however allegedly small, have a long and fascinating regional, and sometimes national, history of their own. Given that most football clubs have their roots in a maternalistic Victorian society it should be no surprise that, like us, 18 of the Conference Premier clubs (or their direct predecessors) have their roots in the Nineteenth Century. As an example, when you step over the threshold into Barnet, Dartford, Gateshead, Nuneaton Town, Woking and even our much maligned neighbours Forest Green Rovers, you are actually stepping into a stirring history that dates back to the same time frame - 1888/1889. Yet we sometimes treat these clubs as if we think they formed a few years ago to have a bit of a run about on some grass, and I could certainly strangle anyone who condescendingly refers to ANY opposition as a 'pub team'.

When you look the other way you will see that 22 current Football League teams are ex-Conference clubs, so we still need to make a hurried departure from this old fashioned thinking that the Football League remains preserved in aspic, where a gentleman's club controls the membership and only lets in 'big' teams. The Third to Fifth tiers are basically a free-for-all now and are the preserve of nobody.

Finally, I was surprised that Darrell went on at length about the alleged anxiety players and management face when Rovers play, that it was a "thankless task" where they expected to "get stick during and after" a loss, which resulted in having "to put the shutters up in the changing room and ignore what is going on outside". I can imagine the atmosphere amongst away fans at Altrincham and Braintree wasn't nice, but they were just two games out of eight. It is not representative of the generally supportive atmosphere they have received. Yes there are critics, and some of them are very vocal, but why should he let them dominate his analysis of how many fans feel about him and the efforts of his squad. As I watch Rovers I don't feel that it is all doom and gloom.

Maybe this is all a clever psychological ploy to provoke a 'them vs. us' motivation. But maybe not. Either way it's a dangerous game to play with paying fans and trigger happy owners.

DI STATS - SUBS

This was the only game of the season when Rovers didn't use any of their substitutes, and three games saw only a solitary sub used (AFC Telford Utd and Wrexham at home, and Dover Athletic away).

Darrell Clarke was usually a fan of using subs though, with all three used in 37 out of the 52 games in the full season.

Rovers never lost in the 15 games where less than three subs were used.

Both Josh Wakefield and Abdulai Baggie spent their entire Rovers 'career' on the bench (or in the stands). Wakefield was on loan for a month from AFC Bournemouth and sat on the bench four times but never got his boot dirty. Baggie was with us for several months at the end of the season but only got on the bench twice, at Macclesfield Town & Dover Athletic, and never got a minute of play; the definition of an insurance policy if ever there was one...

WEEK 21 - ACCENTUATE THE POSITIVE

PUBLISHED ON WEDNESDAY 24TH SEPTEMBER 2014

Tuesday 16th September - Conference

Bristol Rovers 3 **Nuneaton Town 1**

Parkes - 2', Taylor - 48', Dean - 68'
Gosling - 78'

Rovers: Mildenhall, Lockyer, Trotman, Parkes, Brown, Gosling (Clarke - 84'), Mansell (Capt.), Sinclair, Martin, Cunnington (Harrison - 68'), Taylor (White - 89').

Unused Substitutes: Puddy, McChrystal, White.

Attendance: 4,864, inc 65 Boro boys Referee: Craig Hicks

Saturday 20th September - Conference

Bristol Rovers 2 **Woking 0**

Cunnington - 3', Mansell - 86'

Rovers: Mildenhall, Leadbitter, Lockyer, Brown, Gosling [Booked] (Clarke - 45'), Mansell (Capt.), Sinclair, Martin, Cunnington (Harrison - 60'), Taylor (White - 90+').

Unused Substitutes: Puddy, McChrystal.

Attendance: 6,026, inc 276 Cardinals Referee: Adam Bromley

Played 11 Points 20 Position 7th *Gap to leaders [Barnet] = 5 points*

Accentuate the Positive

Nuneaton were the first team we have faced this season who really did look like they we could have played all night and they would never have contrived to beat us. There was a very short period where they may have levelled it at 2-2, but I still feel we might have gone on to win it.

The match reminded me of years gone by when we played non-league teams in the FA Cup (the recent example of Corby Town in 2011 springs to mind, who were too cocky by half), and it always seemed like just a matter of time before we triumphed.

It is nice to see a bit of old fashioned wing play from Dave Martin, although there are times you feel he is a little too overconfident. He reminds me a little of Muzzy Carayol, the last winger to truly excite the Mem. Although Kaid Mohammad and Fabian Broghammer had pace they didn't have the tricks and didn't face up to defenders and take them on head on like Martin does. He pace to burn and when he wasn't in possession many a Nuneaton wide player saw him dash in to nick the ball off them as they dallied. That contribution shouldn't be underestimated; there are plenty of pacy players out there who only ever use their pace going in one direction and won't also use it to defend or harass the opposition into mistakes.

Much has been made of the exaggerated belief that Rovers fans cause anxiety in the stadium and can help the opposition. It's interesting though to note that when looked at from a different angle not everyone sees it like that, and an unbeaten home record seems to suggest the theory smells of bull. Nuneaton Town were clearly a little startled by our support and unwisely tried to play it out from such deep positions that I speculated if the wonderfully entitled Exodus Geohaghon may at one point go and fetch the ball from the Gloucester Road. Woking's 'Mr. Non-League' manager, Garry Hill, praised our support and said we could make it very difficult for any team to get a positive result at the Mem.

Of course we will never fully know how much early goals in both matches have helped, but personally, from the middle of the Blackthorn Terrace, I don't feel this so-called negative atmosphere. Yes there are few collective groans when a pass goes hideously astray, but that is physically very hard to stop. It's a split second human reaction; an exhalation of your life force when you yearn to watch good football but are temporarily disappointed. We had been fed manure for four seasons, so it shouldn't have been a surprise that previous years have witnessed some obnoxious gaseous emissions from the wrong end. There is nothing like wins and goals to settle a crowd down though. Or a bad stomach.

Finally well done to those 65 Nuneaton fans and 230 Wrexham fans who came on a Tuesday night. It may not seem like a lot but any supporter of their local team deserves praise in my book, especially on one of the far too numerous Tuesday night games we have (eight before Christmas).

Southport will be a fascinating clash, and we do have a few connections with them. Although we are on a roll, our away resilience is still unproven as one Lincoln City doesn't make a summer. And given that Southport's home form is entirely erratic, with two wins and three losses, it sounds like no-one is going to be able to predict this one with any certainty.

We've never won at Southport. We have only played the Sandgrounders four times, all in the late 60s and early 70s when they had their only four seasons in the Third Tier, but we lost three and drew one. Only one Pirate, Ray Mabbutt, has ever scored at Haig Avenue and that was in the first ever encounter between us in 1968.

Southport enjoyed 57 years of League football until they were voted out of the League in 1978 after three consecutive 23rd place finishes. Although they had a mere 31 points, Rochdale were 7 points worse off, and had been rock bottom of the table since the fourth game of the season, but it was Southport who failed to get re-elected, letting in a little team called Wigan Athletic from non-league (I wonder where they are now?). They were rather unluckily the last club to leave the League through the re-election process.

Their Salisbury-born boss Martin Foyle is not only a hugely experienced League manager, but was also our first team coach for a very brief period in 2011. His 'crime' was being brought in by Dave Penney, so when Penney was chopped, so was Foyle. In reality this six week sojourn adds about as much spice to Saturday's contest as the gentlest Korma does to an Indian takeaway.

To be blunt there is going to be little spice this season but I for one will quite happily swap a season of blood boiling zing for a succession of ruthlessly efficient two goal wins.

WEEK 22 - TAKE THIS CUP AWAY FROM ME

PUBLISHED ON TUESDAY 30TH SEPTEMBER 2014

Saturday 27th September - Conference

Southport 0

Bristol Rovers 1

Gosling - 13'

Rovers: Mildenhall, Lockyer [Booked], Trotman, Parkes, Brown, Gosling (Clarke - 54'), Sinclair, Mansell (Capt.), Martin (McChrystal - 82'), Taylor, Cunnington (Harrison - 60').

Unused Substitutes: Puddy, White.

Attendance: 1,202, inc 367 Gas Referee: Rob Jones

Played 12 Points 23 Position 4th *Gap to leaders [Barnet] = 5 points*

Take this cup away from me

I'm sorry if I'm late with this week's article but I've been terribly busy lobbying the Conference Premier bigwigs to make sure Darrell Clarke does NOT win the Manager of the Month award for September 2014.

This season the Conference have changed the award from being decided purely on points won, to a more nuanced system involving a panel of judges, so there is a chance my mythical lobbying skills could be effective. This new system was reiterated when the inaugural award, in August 2014, was given to Neil Aspin from FC Halifax Town, even though Martin Allen's Barnet had a slightly better points record.

Before a full round of Tuesday matches Darrell has the joint best record in September, losing just at Braintree Town and winning the other five. Torquay United fans may have thought Chris Hargreaves had the award in the bag after five consecutive wins (all to clean sheets, with 11 goals scored) but a shock defeat on Saturday at whipping boys AFC Telford United put the bucks amongst the gulls. Martin Allen is again only slightly behind. All three clubs have difficult away fixtures on Tuesday, but whatever happens I wouldn't be surprised if Darrell got it anyway, as his five consecutive wins came at a time of great pressure when he was almost going to get the chop. They say that 'when the going gets tough, the tough get going' and that is certainly what Rovers have done this month.

Historical minded Gasheads will know why I don't want Darrell to win it, especially this month of any.

In September 2009 Paul Trollope defied the odds after the timid August loss of the talismanic Rickie Lambert (striker, penalty taker, free kick taker and assist maker all rolled into one), and won four matches out of five, including the celebrated last minute triumph at Rickie's new club, Southampton, our first win there since 1961. The day before our next match, against my best friend's team Norwich City, who were already nine points and six places behind us and had started off disastrously after relegation the season before, Paul was given the poison chalice that no fan wants to see; the dreaded Manager of the Month award, which always seems to be a hot potato when given to smaller clubs.

A 5-1 drubbing saw the wheels fell off our wagon at Norwich, and it set in motion a run of five losses on the trot (all our League games in October), when we leaked 15 goals in the process. By the 24th October Norwich were already above us and the 'natural' order of the world seemed to be restored. It looked like the butterfly who had flapped his wings in Papua New Guinea and caused this chaotic series of events had just been eaten by a lizard. Or a Canary maybe?

My glee at our little club being better than my best friend's jolly (yellow and) green giant had lasted about two months, and after our meeting Norwich went on to plunder an astonishing 47 points from the next 54 available. By the end of the following season we had been dumped into the bottom division and they were going up to the Premier League.

At least it is now looking up for both of our clubs, following simultaneous relegations last season. Five consecutive wins is just what we all needed and without injuries and suspensions, and only five allowed on the bench, our squad is currently looking passable, which is particularly useful considering that Darrell seems to play the players he needs for the changeable tactics he employs rather than just keep the same team each match. This was labelled tinker-ism by some when we were doing badly, but is now seen as a strength when we are flexible enough to adapt to the opposition, and, of course, when it leads to a win!

WEEK 23 - AWAY GAME QUIRKS AND FRONT LINE FIREWORKS

PUBLISHED ON THURSDAY 9TH OCTOBER 2014

Tuesday 30th September - Conference

Eastleigh 1
Collins - 33'

Bristol Rovers 1
Clarke - 52'

Rovers: Mildenhall [Dismissed], Lockyer, Trotman, Parkes [Booked], Brown, Clarke [Dismissed], Mansell (Capt.), Sinclair [Booked], Gosling (Puddy - 31'), Harrison (Martin - 84'), Taylor (Cunnington − 45').

Unused Substitutes: McChrystal, White.

Attendance: 2,621 [their new league record], inc 994 Gas Referee: Colin Lymer

Saturday 4th October - Conference

Bristol Rovers 1
Cunnington - 35'

Dover Athletic 1
Murphy - 90'

Rovers: Puddy, Lockyer, Trotman, Parkes, Brown, Gosling (Monkhouse − 71' [Booked]), Mansell (Capt.), Sinclair, Martin, Cunnington (Harrison − 69'), Taylor.

Unused Substitutes: Preston, McChrystal, White.

Attendance: 6,162, inc 194 almost Frenchies   Referee: Wayne Barratt

Played 14 Points 25 Position 6th *Gap to leaders [Barnet] = 7 points*

Away game quirks and front line fireworks

Eastleigh was what away games are all about, and exactly why I've been getting my head down to edit a book about the marvellous away game memories of Rovers fans.

A new ground for us, a shell shocked pub crammed to the rafters (they thought the pub quiz was supposed to be the big event of the night until we turned up), two sending's off, and an absolutely 'worldie' goal from Ollie Clarke that sent 1,000 Gasheads wild.

Away games dig up the quirks of life that home games often don't. The highs, the lows, the loves, the hates, the times we get lost, wet or hideously late, made some great mates on the journey home, or find the finest beer available to humanity in a tiny little pub.

The metal terrace we were on had recently been purchased from Exeter Chiefs Rugby Club, dragged along the A35 and re-erected next to the famous Capability Brown parkland between Southampton and Eastleigh. The cameraman on a gantry above us reported that the whole stand was rocking with us on it, both aurally and physically. The ground really is along a country lane, which was pitch black for sections, particularly the bit by the graveyard of the Parish church, the devilishly entitled St. Nicks, whose claim to fame is a one handed clock and various memorials to the great and the good, including the tomb of Sir Robert Fleming, one of the judges who tried Guy Fawkes in 1605.

If only our front line were as incendiary...

Everyone had a good laugh, and the Policing and the stewarding was spot-on and focused on safety rather than security. It was nice to see Policemen on bikes at a football match, rather than horses, and stopping traffic to let walking fans have priority.

The Eastleigh chairman even took time out of his busy schedule paying over the odds for ex-League players to write a beautiful open letter thanking Rovers fans for our excellent attitude towards the poor facilities, being an "absolute credit to your club", and allowing Eastleigh to have their "special night", as it was their highest ever crowd for a competitive match.

This love-in didn't quite extend onto the pitch though which saw a combative match which Rovers could have won despite going down to 10 men with only a third of the match gone, and then going behind within a few minutes. We needed to get to half-time as soon as possible. I nudged my mate and said 'Clarke has got to change something. The obvious swap is Cunnington for Taylor.' And so it was, and how it changed the game, along with Lee Brown being pushed up into left wing in a 3-4-2 formation; a bold move when 1-0 down, down to 10 men and away from home. Brown is often wasted as a conventional Left Back, especially when he doesn't have much to do, and I'd love to see 3-5-2 played more often, especially as Lockyer isn't a natural right back. The partnership between the much maligned Ellis Harrison (who was brilliant and did everything expected of him) and Cunnington was neigh on perfect, and I roughly scratched my head when they didn't start together against Dover.

Darrell Clarke completely and utterly out-thought their manager. The one thing that would have caused us a real problem when down to 10 men would have been width, particularly high up the pitch with no full backs. So what did Eastleigh do? Well, nothing really. They didn't adapt, they didn't bring on a winger (we had Dave Martin on the bench, god knows what their silly money had bought them to put on their bench), and they didn't push someone with pace out wide. If the money they've spent buys you a team with no width / no multi-tasking players, then I'd prefer what we've done. They seem to have gone down the route that everyone told us NOT to do; namely, ex-League players on their way down the slippery pyramid.

In this blog precisely six weeks ago I expressed the opinion that we needed an out and out goal scorer, and if necessary we should spend some serious money on him and see it as an investment. It's hardly a unique or a complicated view. In fact Rovers fans of all ages, from those brought up on Geoff Bradford's powerful boot to those who witnessed Rickie Lambert's all round ability, via Jamie Cureton's guile and poise, will know that goal scorers win matches and it is one of the few positions on the pitch where their contribution really can be quantified. Unfortunately they often cost money, even for the lesser known prospects.

For all his alertness and perseverance up front, Matty Taylor simply hasn't scored enough goals, especially when presented with clear chances. When Jamie White signed for us he boldly said that any chance in the box would end up in the back of the net. Admittedly he hasn't been given many chances to prove that, but that promise may end up hollower than a dead tree trunk. I would just love to see Taylor or White stick in a chance within 10 metres of goal very soon.

At the risk of harking back to last week's blog, which focused on the Manager of the Month award and the start of the 2009/10 season, we need to learn the lesson of that season, when, after some early Autumn success, our club erroneously concluded that we had cleverly got away without even attempting to replace Rickie Lambert with a consistently successful goal scorer.

WEEK 24 - DECISIONS, DECISIONS

PUBLISHED ON WEDNESDAY 15TH OCTOBER 2014

Tuesday 7th October - Conference

Bristol Rovers 1   Dartford 0

Taylor (pen) - 37'

Rovers: Mildenhall, Lockyer, Trotman, Parkes, Brown, Sinclair, Clarke, Mansell [Booked] (Capt.), Martin (Monkhouse - 65'), Cunnington, Taylor [Booked] (Harrison - 74').

Unused Substitutes: Puddy, McChrystal, White.

Attendance: 5,112, inc 79 Darts   Referee: Adam Hopkins

Saturday 11th October - Conference

Aldershot Town 2   Bristol Rovers 2

Williams (pen) - 16', Roberts - 77'   Monkhouse - 42', Taylor (pen) - 68'

Rovers: Mildenhall, Lockyer [Booked], Trotman, Parkes (McChrystal - 89'), Brown, Monkhouse (Leadbitter - 68'), Mansell (Capt.), Clarke, Martin, Cunnington (Harrison - 79'), Taylor.

Unused Substitutes: Puddy, White.

Attendance: 3,466 inc 1,255 Gas   Referee: Rob Whitton

Played 16 Points 29 Position 4th   *Gap to leaders [Barnet] = 4 points*

Decisions, Decisions

Aldershot was another excellent away day, despite the below average performance, and has not only increased our unbeaten run to nine matches, but results in us being unbeaten for four away matches in a row. That may not sound marvellous on its own but it is a decent recovery after a solitary point from our first four away games this season, and our pitiable performances last season when we had the worst away record in the League Two, with just 14 points taken from a possible 69 on offer.

It was an entertaining game, and an entertaining crowd on a proper old-school terrace. Not much has changed at The Recreation Ground since my previous visit in 2001, and 1,255 Gasheads utterly overwhelming the funfair catering wagons (one advertised candy floss and a carvery; not quite sure how the later could ever be provided though... photographic evidence is available on page 82) and the tiny toilet - I am not sure if the ladies even had a toilet. Our away support was larger than the entire attendance at 7 out of the 11 other Conference games.

If we can get a draw at a decent team, retain our fourth spot, and come back from behind for the second away game in a row, even when we aren't playing very well, think of what we could potentially achieve when firing on all cylinders. Barnet squandered a 3-0 lead at home, Torquay United have lost three out of their last four, FC Halifax Town have lost two out of their last three, and several of the top teams play each other in the next two rounds of matches. The significance of grinding out results whilst still taking shape as a team should therefore not be under-estimated.

Our midfield was a serious problem on Saturday, although Aldershot must be given credit for the strength of theirs, and their good use of width. Without the livewire Stuart Sinclair we looked seriously weakened in the middle of the park, and not only did the extremely left footed Andy Monkhouse look very rusty on the right wing, but Dave Martin had a shocker on the left wing. I have got excited about Martin in the past but I do wonder if he is the footballing equivalent of the cricketing 'flat track bully', a player who can dominate against the minnows like Nuneaton Town, but struggles when up against better players.

Darrell Clarke has some difficult dilemmas on his hands now. Daniel Leadbitter came on for Monkhouse and injected some youthful pace into the right midfield/wing position. Although he may have been a right back for Hereford United, Darrell doesn't seem to trust him there, as his attacking prowess outweighs his defensive ability. To some degree the same can be said of Lee Brown, who is rather wasted as a conventional full back, so another try of a 3-5-2 formation in the near future would be interesting. Given that Tom Lockyer is not really a right back we are still stuck in that classic scenario that when your best player for many years leaves you (right back Michael Smith) it seems to be doubly difficult to find a replacement.

Whatever happens Darrell will be forced into a change this Saturday as one of the portents of Lockyer's weakness at right back has already come home to roost; five yellow cards for poor tackles, leading to a one match suspension. I like utility players, but I don't like players out of position. There is a difference.

Fans have debated whether the goal shy Matty Taylor should be dropped, or maybe moved out towards the wing, to see if his excellent approach play could be useful there. I would actually be interested to see him 'in the hole' / a number 10, with a goal scorer ahead of him, although I appreciate that accommodating such a position can be fiendishly complicated, especially when dealing with players who after all are deemed only good enough for the fifth tier of football.

One thing that would help our team dominate games more would be cutting out unforced errors. Without wishing to dissect the past too much, lazy passes like Tom Parkes' at Eastleigh need to be curtailed. On Saturday these errors included a handball and a totally unnecessary free kick given away in a very dangerous position, which lead to a lovely curled equaliser from the Shots. Fans are sometimes too quick to blame the refereeing at this level, which admittedly is hideous, although expected, rather than questioning the decision making of our own players.

WEEK 25 - MAKE HAY WHILST THE SUN SHINES

PUBLISHED ON WEDNESDAY 22ND OCTOBER 2014

Saturday 18th October - Conference

Bristol Rovers 0　　　　　　**Forest Green Rovers 1**

　　　　　　　　　　　　　　　　Coles - 15'

Rovers: Mildenhall, Leadbitter [Dismissed], Trotman [Booked], Parkes, Brown, Monkhouse (Martin - 22'), Clarke (White - 84'), Mansell [Booked] (Capt.), Gosling, Cunnington, Taylor (Harrison - 65').

Unused Substitutes: Puddy, McChrystal.

Attendance: 7,014 inc 362 foresters　　Referee: Lee Swabey (2nd time this season)

Played 17 Points 29 Position 6th　*Gap to leaders [Barnet] = 7 points*

Make Hay Whilst the Sun Shines

I'm getting rather bored writing this, but for the third time this season I need to write about getting a goal scorer in the team, or at least letting one of the fringe players have a chance to prove themselves up front. Failing those we could even, fitness willing, try Andy Monkhouse up front. Try something please. Anything! Just like never properly replacing Rickie Lambert, or failing to recruit a goal scorer last season, this situation is not going to just magically disappear like a Paul Daniel's tribute act. Do we like this? Not a lot.

Saturday's F.A. Cup visit to Dorchester Town could be the perfect time to make some changes and let Ellis Harrison or Jamie White start upfront and see what they can do. Ellis combined brilliantly with Adam Cunnington in the second half at Eastleigh, yet that partnership has inexplicably never been tried from the start of a game. Talk of Ellis being 'better suited' as an impact sub seems to defy all modern logic to me. This is the 2010's. Football is a very different game to when players played on quagmires, ate pie and chips before the game, had a fag after it, and David Fairclough was the original super sub for Liverpool. Why should a fit young man with pace and presence be consigned to an almost endless Groundhog Day cameo?

Don't get me wrong, I'm not suggesting Harrison is the panacea to end all our problems (he may well start against the Magpies and miss a sitter), but I can't see how continuing to start with a STRIKER who doesn't score goals is a positive message to his team mates who must be itching to prove that they could do better, and wince when watching this continual failure from the subs bench, or even worse, the stands.

However, I wouldn't be surprised if Darrell Clarke prefers to let Matty Taylor start yet again in the vain hope that a goal or two against lower division opposition will give him a confidence boost.

I remember the moment Matty Taylor scored his one and only goal from open play this season, whilst we were enjoying our 'easiest' win of the season against a Nuneaton Town side with a predilection for suicidal catenaccio style passing around their deep back line. Whilst their attempt was thoroughly admirable, it was as misguided as an attempt to walk to the North Pole in flip-flops and budgie smugglers. Matty's neat goal led to an instant reaction of a few mouths on the terrace, and later several fingers on forum keyboards, along the lines of 'well, that shut his critics up', as if no-one was allowed to politely point out that strikers should regularly score goals. The floodgates never did open of course, and with only two penalties since, Matty Taylor still shows little ability to actually put away the decent chances that are regularly coming his way.

The reality of course is that most so-called 'critics' are not trying to be unkind, or personal, but to concentrate efforts on the rafter in the eye when others are too busy focusing on the tiny blades of straw elsewhere.

Thinking of straw, my old Wiltshire dad would have said that the best time to make hay was whilst the sun shined. And the best time to strengthen your squad is when you are buoyant, not after you've suffered a sticky patch, which 1 win in 5 games could be now be considered. Of course it's not a bad run per se, but in order to have any chance of keeping up with the Jones, or more accurately the Bees, or the Cardinals, we have to win more games and to do that we need to take our chances. There is a mini-crisis of confidence going on at the moment, with the midfield being bypassed by long balls over their heads. Given that Darrell says he doesn't want to play that way, we can only conclude that poor distribution from the back, the lack of a 'water carrier' in the middle, and maybe a lack of faith in the ability of the midfield, is causing this dreary occurrence.

Any regular fan will know we have been grinding out results rather than putting any teams to the sword, and the margins have been too tight to conclude that our squad is complete. Indeed we have only won two games by more than one goal, and have a goal difference of merely +4, which is the second worst in the entire top 12. Thinking of that number, we are now only three points above 12th position.

Our right hand side is currently a real problem, and although whoever is chosen to play out there is trying their hardest, they are always playing out of position. Tom Lockyer isn't a right back, Stuart Sinclair isn't a right winger, Andy Monkhouse is exceptionally left footed, and Daniel Leadbitter looks like more of a winger, or a wing-back, than a right back. The later 'problem' could be a blessing in disguise though; give him a game as a winger, and get a decent defender in to cover behind him.

WEEK 26 - TO STARE INTO SOME SPRING

PUBLISHED ON SATURDAY 1ST NOVEMBER 2014

Saturday 25th October - FA Cup 4th Qualifying Round

Dorchester Town 1

Walker - 50'

Bristol Rovers 7

Monkhouse - 17' & 85', Taylor - 19',
Mansell - 47', Harrison - 52', 79' & 90'

Rovers: Mildenhall, Lockyer, Trotman (McChrystal), Parkes, Monkhouse, Clarke, Mansell (Capt.) (Thomas), Brown, Gosling, Harrison, Taylor (White - 63').

Unused Substitutes: Puddy, Martin, Cunnington.

Attendance: 1,909 inc 1,139 Gas   Referee: Dean Treleaven

To Stare into Some Spring

I was really pleased to see a few changes to the team on Saturday, which resulted in an uber efficient 7-1 drubbing of Dorchester Town. Admittedly they usually play two divisions below us, but nothing can be taken for granted in football, and our ex-Landlords Bath City are most probably still shell shocked at being thumped by the same score away to East Thurrock United, who play a division below them.

I'm not so narcissistic as to think that a man with almost 500 professional football appearances under his belt, and 4 1/2 years in football management has read my little column, but it was nice to see last week's blog come true, with Ellis Harrison and Andy Monkhouse up front, and Lee Brown given a more forward role on the left. I'm not sure how many times Darrell will be able to play 3-4-3 or 3-5-2 in a league match, but they certainly seem like systems that suit our current squad as Brown and Leadbitter are wasted as conventional full backs, and Tom Lockyer isn't one either. Monky is also a proven goal scorer, with over 75 career goals from less than 500 appearances, and his unusually tall frame for a 'winger' gives him a more than useful presence in the box that is also slightly wasted when playing very wide. Being left footed can also potentially give balance to the forward line.

It was also pleasing to see that the midfield were not regularly being by-passed by long balls over their heads. Of course the quality of the opposition

helped, but all in all it must do wonders for your confidence and togetherness when everyone has a good day at the office.

So far, so good then. The only worry of course is that, just like our excellent
start to the 2009/10 season after losing Rickie Lambert in August, seven
goals could help sweep our Conference Premier goal tally of 20 in 17 matches
under the carpet, the joint lowest in the top half of the table. I sincerely
hope we still look out for a goal scorer, especially as Adam Cunnington will
be forced to return to Cambridge United when his loan expires towards the
end of November.

The news that recently resigned Rovers Director (and Chairman for some
time) Geoff Dunford is writing his memoirs of being a big cheese at BRFC
comes as vaguely interesting news if you care about the infantile politics of
football.

Unlike many Rovers fans, who seem to have very robust, and polarised,
opinions of Geoff, I have not met him and have no strong judgment of him
as a man, a Board member or as a leader.

I do however wonder if a truly humble man would feel the need to write his
own version of history, and to announce it barely a few months after his
protracted departure, which unfortunately finally coincided with the lowest
point in Rovers' history (so far?). Mr. Dunford wrote on social media that,
"My 30 years at Bristol Rovers need to be recorded factually so have decided
to write a book warts and all! Time to put the record straight!" and later
elaborated on his inspiration; "Fed up with other people telling the world
what I did and didn't do... It will put to bed the rubbish and misinformation
on social media... It is better to be honest and let people judge for themselves. ". Yes, and likewise I'll let you readers also make your own mind up
about this project.

It seems worthy to note that his father, Denis, did not feel the desire to write
about his time at Rovers, even though he was the man who is widely credited
as 'saving' Rovers in the mid 1980's and helping mastermind our stellar
period in the late 1980s and early 1990s. Maybe the difference is that a book
by Denis could have automatically become a hagiography, whereas Geoff's
presumably cannot.

WEEK 27 - AN UNDISCIPLINED MIND
LEADS TO SUFFERING

PUBLISHED ON MONDAY 10TH NOVEMBER 2014

Saturday 1st November - Conference

AFC Telford United 0   Bristol Rovers 1

Clarke - 50'

Rovers: Puddy, Lockyer, Trotman (McChrystal - 39' [Booked]), Parkes, Monkhouse [Dismissed], Clarke, Mansell (Capt.), Brown, Gosling [Booked], Harrison (Cunnington - 72'), Taylor [Booked].

Unused Substitutes: Martin, White, Wilson.

Attendance: 2,860 inc 895 Gas   Referee: Ryan Johnson

Played 18 Points 32 Position 4th   *Gap to leaders [Barnet] = 10 points [Barnet played 1 game extra]*

An undisciplined mind leads to suffering

After a fifth red card in 19 games, and Tom Lockyer's one match ban for five yellow cards, you could be left wondering if our players have a discipline problem, and whether the resultant bans are costing us dearly.

Although a closer look suggests we don't have an institutional crisis, or a team of dirty hackers, it is not a record to be proud of and it could well cause us problems if we continue in this vein. We have by far the worst record of the better teams in the division. In fact the other nine teams in the top ten have only received eight red cards between them, and Barnet, Gateshead and Woking have not had any. Last season the runaway winners of the division, Luton Town, only had one all season, and despite receiving 60 yellows, they shared them around their large squad so they had no problems with suspensions. Cambridge United, the other success story of last season, picked up only eight yellows in their first 20 games and were heralded by the F.A., who commented, almost Dalai Lama-esque, that, "The best behaved teams are the ones with the most disciplined coaches".

Three of our reds have been received very late in the match and have not affected the game at all. The impact has therefore been more keenly felt via the resultant suspension. Stuart Sinclair was sent packing in the 90th minute at Altrincham for maybe wisely denying them the chance to heap more misery on us (our first loss to a 'minnow' was hard enough to take; but three goals may have been meltdown time), Ollie Clarke rather witlessly managed two yellows within injury time at Eastleigh, and last weekend Andy Monkhouse was sent off with just three minutes left, and we still won, although we did collect three more yellows during a frantic two minute blast of 'backs to the wall' injury time.

Only Steve Mildenhall's alleged trip outside the box at Eastleigh was early in the game, the 29th minute, and the resultant change of personnel and formation at half-time to three at the back actually saw us play better, and rescue a point, with sub Adam Cunnington forming a partnership with Ellis Harrison which changed the game.

We will never quite know how much Daniel Leadbitter's 59th minute slip / lunge against Forest Green Rovers may have affected our ability to grab a point back, but it surely contributed to ending our nine game unbeaten run and handing a promotion rival three vital points. This red though was happily one of only two out of the five to be deemed violent conduct and thus result in a three match ban .

Tom Lockyer's one match ban for five yellow cards was slightly surprising in view of the stats believing that he's only committed eight fouls in his 17 games (Dave Martin is top of the fouls table with 23 in 15 games, but has no bookings) and in general our defence have been very 'clean' this season. Amazingly our solid central defensive partnership of Neal Trotman and Tom Parkes (who have played 16 out of the 19 games together) only have four yellows between them, and left back Lee Brown has none, and only five fouls, despite being an ever present so far. I hope these stats are the result of being clean tacklers rather than challenge shirkers!

I would suggest that the bans haven't yet caused us serious problems partly because we've had so few injuries and because they've been well spaced out, but more importantly they haven't on the whole touched most of the first names on the team sheet. One strength of our squad is that whilst we only have a few stand-out players, we do have several players who can slot into vacant positions with a minimum of fuss.

But one weakness is also precisely that we only have a few stand-out players. The players who pick themselves seem to be Steve Mildenhall (although Will Puddy is probably better at distribution and crosses), Neal Trotman, Tom Parkes, Lee Brown, Lee Mansell, and Stuart Sinclair. The rest, to me, are much of a muchness.

Matty Taylor and Lee Mansell are both currently on four yellow cards each, and will face a one match ban if they pick up another by the 30th November. Although this is hardly a positive state of affairs, it is mitigated by the consideration that they have only missed one match between them all season, and that we've already ploughed through six midweek games. Reaching those five cards though would put pressure on the team, and if Taylor reaches his five I imagine we will look back and wonder what on earth the point was as he's hardly needed to make any game saving challenges or to 'take one for the team'!

Statistics of course are merely statistics, and watching the game is probably more important, but they do give an indication of where potential problems lie, and this is certainly one problem of our own making, and therefore offers a rare opportunity to have some control over attempting to improve it. To gain automatic promotion from any league, but especially the sole slot in the Conference Premier, requires an almost perfect season, where injuries and suspensions are kept to a minimum.

Let's hope we can do both.

WEEK 28 - 1 COULD BE A MILLIONAIRE IF 1 HAD THE MONEY

PUBLISHED ON WEDNESDAY 12TH NOVEMBER 2014

Saturday 8th November - FA Cup 1st Round

Tranmere Rovers 1   **Bristol Rovers 0**

Power (pen) - 54'

Rovers: Mildenhall, Lockyer, McChrystal (Capt.) (Cunnington - 82'), Parkes, Brown, Gosling (Della-Verde - 58'), Sinclair, Mansell, Martin (Harrison - 68'), Brunt, Taylor.

Unused Substitutes: Puddy, Thomas, Wilson, White.

Attendance: 3,559 inc 340 Gas   Referee: Darren England

I could be a millionaire if I had the money

It is often said that in Cup games a team near the top of one division will be favourites to beat a team struggling in the division above. I would generally tend to subscribe to that view as well, as success tends to breed success, and equally doom and gloom tends to create anxiety and negativity.

There is also a prevalent feeling that the gap between League Two and the top half of the Conference Premier is not substantial. Of the last 10 teams to be promoted (barring last season as it's too early to tell), only one has since been relegated back to non-league (Torquay United), and even they enjoyed two play-off slots in their four seasons in League Two.

Crawley Town and Stevenage Borough have been the two high flyers of course, coming from no league history at all and both gaining back-to-back promotions from the Conference, through League Two without stopping, and into League One. Crawley have since finished tenth and 15th in League One. Stevenage were even more successful at the start, finishing sixth in their first League One season, but then struggled for the next two, finishing 18th and then bottom. Fleetwood Town haven't been far behind as after saying goodbye to the Conference in 2012 they finished 13th and fourth in League Two, going into League One via the play-offs.

Clockwise from left – 1) Flood-lights AND a rainbow at The Hive, Barnet's new ground. 2 & 3) Director Parking at Braintree Town, along side York Road (Maidenhead United) style toilets. 4) Advert for our first ever visit to Altricham – they had the last laugh on the pitch though. 5) Daisy Wilton on her way back from her first ever Gas match, at Alty, and amazingly still a happy little Gashead.

Photos kindly supplied by – 1, 2 & 3 = Matthew Foster / 4 = Dan Lovering / 5 = Simon Wilton.

Clockwise from left –
1) Gas terrace at the Sandgrounders (Southport).
2) Lovely evening & cracking
atmosphere at Eastleigh.
3) The carvery & candy floss
were strangely out of stock at
Aldershot – BTW the queue on
the left side is for the lone
portatoilet being shared by
1,255 Pirates. 4) I was in this
very long & slightly depressed
walk out at the Shots, where a
draw felt more like a loss.

Photos kindly supplied by – 1 =
Sean Williams / 2 = Joe GasHead Esq.
/ 3 = Martin Bull / 4 = Chris Power.

Clockwise from top left −
1) Tam Johnson at Telford with Rovers stalwart Sheila H in background.
2) Lee Mansell, MOTM vs. Welling United, getting a hug from honoured guest Christian McClean.
3) Rovers' 5−a−side team, captained by 'The Beard'.
4) Life was rarely easy being a Rovers fan until about Spring, so shining mobile phone lights provided plenty of distraction at several winter games, including Torquay on NYD.
5) Four gorgeous munchkins, (L to R) Thomas, Henry, Jayden & Oscar presenting Lee Mansell with his Fan's Forum Sponsor Club MOTM bubbly vs. Welling Utd.

Photos kindly supplied by −
1 = David Johnson / 2 = Sean Williams / 3 = Mark Lewis / 4 = Rick Weston / 5 = Fan's Forum Sponsor Club.

Clockwise from left –
1) Nuneaton Town was generally accepted as the coldest, foggiest match of the season. 2) No book should be without the obligatory pile of ticket stubs. 3) International Beard Convention at Woking. 4) Looking towards the locked out Gas at the same match – obviously forgot their beards... 5) Pirates packed along the thin terrace whilst a Woking section is empty. Go figure.

Photos kindly supplied by – 1 & 2 = Joe GasHead Esq. / 3 = Ashley Perry / 4 = Matthew Foster / 5 = Dan Lovering.

Dartford special — Above — left — A great following and some great flags (photo by Dan Lovering) — **right —** Mildy playing 'spot the blade of grass' (photo by Sean Williams / Clevedon Gas)

Above — left — Freddie Williams presenting Mark McChrystal with his MOTM award vs Braintree Town (photo by Sean Williams) — **right —** The 'Gateshead International Stadium' was the rather unlikely setting for the third largest capacity in the Conference (photo by Joe GasHead Esq.)

Left — FranceGas easily wins most exotic photo of the book award. Yeah, and biggest show-off of the book award as well! Sadly a massive earthquake hit this stunning area of Nepal only three weeks later. Photo kindly supplied by Colin Emmitt.

Above — Silkmen special (photos by @partizanbristle) — **left** — Hmmm, Moss Rose's away end could do with a revamp... Just like the Mem I guess — **right** — Proper old boy Northern entertainment. No Blue Flames allowed.

Below — Kitey, Clarkey and Stewie — A truly great Rovers bench vs. Chester (photo by Rick Weston)

Above left — The player EVERYONE wanted to meet. 'The Beard' with Cameron & Evie Church, & Oscar Lewis (photo by Russ Church)   **Below** — Gas trip to CE Sabadell in Spain, and proof that blue and red can sometimes get along! Those in red are actually Osasuna fans, their opponents that day (photos by Karen Whitlow)

Kiddie Special – Above – Old skool terrace scenes as Ellis Harrison scored the crucial opening goal – **Below** – At least 2,619 Gas were there, cheering their team onto the pitch. (photos by Dan Lovering)

Dover Special @ The Cricketers – Above right – Fantastic pre match atmosphere, before the heartbreaking finale (photo by Chris Power) – **Below** – Yes sonny, you know where you can stick that drum... (photo by Dan Lovering)

Left – Standing room only before the last game of the season (photo by Sean Williams)

Below Left – Gasheads on the 'away' terrace at the Mem (vs. Alfreton Town) may prove to be an historic sight (photo by @partizanbristle)

Below Left – Rovers line-up vs. Alfreton Town – Put those thighs away Ellis! (photo by Rick Weston)

Left – Pre-match huddle before the FGR Play-Off Semi-Final (photo by Dan Lovering)

Below Left – Someone at Lawford's Gate must be a Gashead (photo by Rick Weston)

Below – Sheila & Brian Oliver attended every home game but had already booked a holiday for mid-May, so had to endure Wembley in different way (photo supplied by Wendi Williams)

Oxford United have been consistently, if rather laboriously, strong (12th, ninth, ninth & eighth) and Burton Albion have been a slow burning sensation (13th, 19th & 17th, but then fourth & sixth). York City are up and down like the Assyrian Empire; a difficult first season in 17th, but a late play-off slot last season via seventh position, and currently back to struggling. Mansfield Town and Newport County rode some patchy form last season to finish their inaugural seasons back in the league 11th and 14th respectively. Only the phoenix from the flames (AFC Wimbledon) has consistently struggled, and also waned, finishing 16th, 20th & 20th.

The F.A. Cup First Round results at the weekend have therefore led to an interesting conundrum, because teams from our division mainly failed against teams in higher divisions.

Runaway leaders Barnet were soundly beaten at home to Wycombe Wanderers (although a sending off just before half-time didn't help), Grimsby Town lost at home to struggling Oxford United, and we of course lost at Tranmere Rovers, who are in the League Two relegation zone.

Braintree Town were thumped 6-0 by Chesterfield, Forest Green Rovers lost to Scunthorpe United, and FC Halifax Town lost to local rivals Bradford City. These three were also all at home, although they were admittedly facing teams two leagues above them.

Only Dover Athletic (a win at home against Morecambe), Chester (a win away at Southend United), Aldershot (a draw at Pompey), and Southport (a draw at Dagenham & Redbridge) can be happy with their days work.

As a fully paid up member of the worriers club, these results, particularly our own, well... worry me. I realise I probably shouldn't think too much about the day we get back into League Two, but it's a bit disconcerting that we couldn't even draw at a poor League Two team who hadn't won since August! As before, the elephant in the room is creating goal scoring opportunities and then taking them. Numerous intelligent Rovers fans came back from the Wirral and to a man they said that Rovers played 'well' and should have got at least a draw.

Yes. But without being too picky I don't totally understand how you can lose and still be described as playing 'well' and, by some, as 'deserving to win'. Surely it's like a golfer who is brilliant with the woods and irons, but who can't putt for toffee, or a darts player who racks up 180's and then misses all his doubles. Putting and check outs are an integral part of those games and poor performance at the end surely negates any strength in the build up play.

The game of football operates at both ends of the pitch, not just one and no-one 'deserves' to win. You either outscore your opponents and win, or you don't. We may well have a parsimonious defence (the fourth tightest in the League), but until we score more goals and comprehend how to unleash the attacking potential of our defenders, such as Lee Brown and Daniel Leadbitter, then I feel we cannot be considered to be playing especially 'well' just because we never leak goals. Any team with a flat back four, an excellent shot stopper, and two relatively defensive central midfielders should expect, as a minimum, to be miserly at the back.

Apparently we would be top of the league if we scored more goals. Yes, and as Clifford. T. Ward sang, "I could be a millionaire if I had the money".

Maybe we simply aren't playing the attacking football that Darrell promised? His substitutions and occasional formation changes are generally positive and certainly not defensive, but that is slightly different than actually being overtly attacking as a team or as an ethos. Having an attacking midfielder in the squad, plus dribbling wingers, or rampaging wing backs, could be considered overtly attacking though, and would be something I'd pay good money to see.

WEEK 29 - MAN UP TO THE JOB!?

PUBLISHED ON FRIDAY 21ST NOVEMBER 2014

Tuesday 11th November - Conference

Alfreton Town 0   **Bristol Rovers 0**

Rovers: Mildenhall, Lockyer, McChrystal (Capt.), Parkes, Leadbitter (Martin – 68'), Mansell, Sinclair, Brown, Taylor, Brunt (Harrison – 60'), White (Della-Verde – 68').

Unused Substitutes: Puddy, Cunnington.

Attendance: 880 inc 315 Gas   Referee: Richard Wigglesworth

Saturday 15th November - Conference

Bristol Rovers 1   **Kidderminster Harriers 1**

Taylor - 83'   Blissett - 67'

Rovers: Mildenhall, Lockyer, McChrystal (Capt.), Parkes, Brown, Della Verde, Mansell, Sinclair, Martin (Taylor - 46'), Brunt (Harrison - 61'), White (Clarke - 46'

Unused Substitutes: Puddy, Balanta.

Attendance: 5,848 inc 287 Carpetmen Referee: Brett Huxtable (2nd time this season)

Played 20 Points 34 Position 4th *Gap to leaders [Barnet] = 11 points [Barnet played 1 game extra]*

Man up to the job!?

After Darrell Clarke's emotional statements about a minuscule minority of negative Rovers fans at the weekly press briefing last Thursday it is amazing how much difference a question mark or an exclamation mark can make to a headline. The headline above comes from a thread on a Rovers Internet forum, although that one didn't have any punctuation. However, if I write 'Man up to the job!' it suggests I am telling Darrell to suck up this negativity and get on with the job he is paid to do, whereas using a question mark will maybe start a debate as to whether he is the right man for the job, to which the answer would mainly be positive.

At the risk of repeating myself I have solidly supported Darrell right from the start, even through relegation, which I don't feel can be pinned on him. To be exact though, I fully support the principles on which he is trying to lead this team, rather than every decision he makes, and every tactic he employs on the pitch.

Overall I think he's doing a good job and in the long run this fresh approach will give us a chance of getting ourselves back to being a well run club. However, I do feel he got last Thursday's press briefing seriously wrong and again revealed a very thin skin for a professional football manager (and ex-player) and an emotional temperament which could be a problem in the future. Fans may have appreciated him weeping on the pitch in the relegation aftermath, and manfully then accepting full responsibility for relegation even though it was clearly not justified, but later they would have been confused by his unusually frank talk about John Ward and the attitude of some of the players last season. Although such honesty is refreshing, and I agree that those outlooks needed to change, it does suggest he's on an emotional roller coaster, and is more in the vein of the occasionally successful Kevin Keegan than the continually successful Alex Ferguson. There are of course numerous reasons Fergie was more successful than the permed one, but a tougher, more consistent persona was certainly one of them.

After his latest grievances a few hundred uber rational Gasheads will hold their chins like Rodin's 'The Thinker' and conclude that 'he's right to wash the dirty linen in public, because we fans need to be told how the staff and players feel, and abuse needs to be tackled head-on', but I'm pretty sure that thousands of decent Gasheads will feel as though it is yet another avoidable affront to all the mature, level headed Gasheads who are fed up with being tarred and feathered by association with a tiny minority of fans who are afflicted with very extreme opinions and unpleasant manners.

Complaining about negativity by talking and acting negatively seems a strange way to encourage positivity. I don't need to hear negativity about a few pea brains. I want to hear positivity about the 5,000+ Gasheads who regularly pay their hard earnt money to watch and support the team, and the staggering average of 751 Gasheads who have travelled to each away game this season, at an average distance of 130 miles a game, to make up 32% of the total crowds.

My Mum says 'If you can't say anything nice, don't say anything at all', which almost sounds like a line from Forrest Gump. Of course this is the mantra the strangely over the top 'fans' should have remembered when even contemplating going on the team bus at Braintree and Alfreton and spouting negative bile at the team they 'support', but equally it could have been something that Darrell may have liked to ponder upon.

I can't see any benefit from suddenly revealing that negative posters were plastered around the training ground, something that not even gossipy forums had heard about. Not only does this secret go back to the start of the season when emotions were high, but it may not have even been perpetrated by a Rovers 'fan' of any description.

I also can't see any benefit from walking out of the weekly press call before taking questions. This is Bristol Rovers in the fifth tier of football, not a highly charged conference to stop war in South Sudan.

But what I find most disappointing is that he has repeated the melodramatic belief that "it does feel at times that it is us against the world", and that maybe they need to "build a sanctuary for the players". This could be quite effective if he takes the fans along for the ride, in a Millwall-esque 'No-one likes us we don't care' type mentality, but the "us against the world" statement seems to be referring to 'players/staff vs. fans', which is really not helpful to anyone.

Our football is still mainly a working class diversion, and as befits a major cosmopolitan city with docks and large areas of serious deprivation, we cannot expect the happy clapping atmosphere of a genteel tourist town, and should be able to be rest confident that our well paid manager gets on with his job and leaves us fans alone to scratch around to find the cash to pay for the slightly better than mediocre canteen fare we are currently being dished up with.

I still support Rovers, I still support Darrell, and I still support the team, but I do sometimes wish for less talk and more action.

WEEK 30 - BRISTOL ROVERS - THE GRAVEYARD OF MANAGERS

PUBLISHED ON THURSDAY 27TH NOVEMBER 2014

Saturday 22nd November - Conference

Chester 2
Oates - 68', Hughes - 70'

Bristol Rovers 2
Blissett - 51', Parkes - 58'

Rovers: Mildenhall, Brown, Lockyer [Booked], McChrystal (Capt.), Parkes, Mansell, Monkhouse, Sinclair, Blissett (Goldberg - 87'), Taylor (Harrison - 77'), Della Verde (Gosling - 66').

Unused Substitutes: Clarke, Balanta.

Attendance: 2,936 inc 497 Gas   Referee: The BBC reported that it was 'Karl Evans' but the BRFC programme says it was 'Wayne Barrett'.

Played 21 Points 35 Position 6th *Gap to leaders [Barnet] = 11 points [Barnet played 1 game extra]*

Bristol Rovers - The Graveyard of Managers

I chuckled on Saturday when one irate Rovers fan demanded Darrell Clarke be sacked for suffering the ignominy of getting a draw at a team who hadn't lost at home since early September.

Since I started supporting Rovers in 1989, we've tended to get our managerial appointments spectacularly right, such as Gerry Francis [first time], Trolls and Lawrence, John Ward [first time], and Ian Holloway to a degree, or spectacularly wrong, such as Ray Graydon, Martin Dobson, Mark McGhee, Garry Thompson... I think I'll stop now.

I'm not quite sure what we do to them, but we have an unerring knack of being the last 'proper' hands-on management job for many of our ex-managers, as if we've reduced them to a gibbering wreck in the corner of the room.

'Player power' famously helped oust **Martin Dobson** in 1991 and also **Dave Penney** two decades later, propelling them both into the record books as the two shortest lived permanent Rovers managers ever (merely 12 and 13 games respectively). I dearly hope that this dubious honour is never allowed to transpire again. Results for both were admittedly disastrous, but it is still nothing for Rovers to be proud of that Dobson had been allowed five years to steadily improve Bury, and we gave him a mere 12 games. Penney similarly is regarded as a legend at Doncaster Rovers, with his five years including back-to-back promotions to take them from the Conference to the Third Tier. Dobson never managed again, preferring to mainly be in the background at Burnley, his foremost club during a very successful playing career, and Penney set up the Dave Penney Football Academy before last year re-emerging back into the game, preferring to get out of the firing line and be an assistant manager at Southend United.

Malcolm Allison was already 65 years old when he came to Twerton in Autumn 1992, almost 30 years since his first managerial job at Bath City. He was allegedly appointed to 'help out' Dennis Rofe, whose promotion from his coaching role the year before was a popular decision following a long caretaker/interim spell that put some old fashioned stability back into the club after the Dobson disaster. Not surprisingly the city wasn't big enough for the both of them, and it was Dennis who drew the short straw. Big Mal couldn't do much better and lasted only 18 games. Dennis returned to coaching and made a long career of it, and Big Mal also never managed again and after long battles with alcohol, domestic problems, depression and, later, dementia sadly died in 2010.

Gerry Francis's return for Rovers' first ever season in the Fourth Tier (2001/02) proved the old adage to 'never go back'. There was no way of covering up that we had a poor squad and a lot of psychological baggage from the historic relegation in May 2001, and not even King Gerry could do much to annul that. Gerry resigned just in time to spend Christmas not needing to worry about football, and has never managed again, preferring media work and coaching, usually for Tony Pulis.

Garry Thompson's record is so bad on paper that it's no surprise he never managed again. He does however have the distinction of being Brentford's only ever 'manager' to boast an unbeaten record, courtesy of a lone draw at Blackpool in March 2004 as their caretaker following the sacking of Wally Downes. As the Bees had not won in over two months, and had lost their last five games, it was probably the best result of his awful career, after Rovers' famous 3-1 thrashing of Derby County in the F.A. Cup in January 2001, the first time a bottom division team had beaten a Premier League incumbent. He was later a part-time Assistant Manager at Conference North side Hucknall Town for less than a year, combining his position with a full-time role in promotions. Recently he became a consultant at a Sports Management agency.

Ray Graydon was a successful coach for almost two decades before finally agreeing to be a manager, where he twice led Walsall into the Championship, and once was second only to Alex Ferguson in the League Managers Association's poll for Manager of the Season. In Uncle Ray's first season with us, 2002/03, Rovers were constantly in the bottom five from early November onwards and were only 'rescued' by the most dramatic Easter resurrection since a certain fellow two Millennia previously. Andy Rammell may have only played seven games for us and scored only in those three crucial wins, but we would have been goners without even half of those 10 points from the last four games of the season.

I call him 'Uncle' as a term of endearment, as he really reminded me of a gentle, courteous Wiltshire uncle. I should know as I have six of them, from a brood of 12. Life at Rovers seemed to knock the stuffing totally out of him, as he has hardly even dabbled with roles in football since his contract was mutually terminated in January 2004.

Ian Atkins was a man often viewed as dislikeable, but a tough manager who stopped the rot of the early Noughties and whose squad became the backbone of the wondrous double finalists of 2006/07. He only managed once more after leaving us, doing an excellent emergency job at Torquay United to save them from relegation in 2006, but was replaced after only 29 games, and turned down an offer to be Director of Football instead. Since then he has worked as a Chief Scout in Europe for Sunderland and Everton.

In an interview he said "I had three or four clubs asking for my services. I chose Bristol Rovers over clubs from a higher division because I thought they were a big club with potential to get to the Championship, with a great fan base, but it was a big mistake. .. The board was split and I was caught in the middle. It is a fantastic club with great fans, but I wish I had never gone there."

Many Rovers fans always felt **Paul Trollope** was more of a coach than a manager / tactician, so it's also no complete surprise that he has only taken coaching jobs since being sacked in December 2010.

A certain Robin Michael Lawrence is one of a select few managers to have managed over 1,000 games, although he hasn't done so since Cardiff City in

2005. He is better known to us as **'Lennie' Lawrence**. Since his existence as Director of Football at Rovers it is not surprising that he has never gone back to being a manager, preferring several consultancy, technical director and assistant manager roles, before recently becoming unemployed again.

Not surprisingly, given the abject failure at his last two managerial jobs (Aberdeen and us) **Mark McGhee** says he feels... "unfulfilled as a manager so I still have things to do". Presumably the things on his 'to do' list are to find out what a few wins feel like? When in an abysmal slump at the Dons Mark famously told reporters, "Go and look me up on Wikipedia. I've got a track record". Yes, that is exactly what our Board of Directors did and precisely how he got our job!

Mark is currently licking his wounds as the Assistant Manager to the Scottish national team, under his old mate Gordon Strachan, and showed great enthusiasm for his job when he remarked that "I imagined that I would spend my whole life managing in the Premier League and I haven't, so I still have things to do and getting an opportunity at this level is okay."

I believe that Darrell Clarke will be seen as a very good appointment in the long run, but if something does happen I somehow don't suspect that Martin Dobson or Ray Graydon are standing by their phones each time the Rovers managerial merry-go-round is cranked up and roaring to go.

QI STATS - KIDDIE CULL

The FA Cup exit on the Wirral, a tame draw at Alfreton Town and looking toothless at home to Kidderminster Harriers seemed to be the final straws that broke the camels back for Darrell Clarke.

All three players who were subbed off against Kiddie (Ryan Brunt, Jamie White & Dave Martin) never played one more league minute for Rovers ever again. Only Dave Martin featured again in the quarters, and that was in the humbling FA Trophy defeat to Bath City, his final appearance for us.

WEEK 31 - TOGETHER EVERYONE ACHIEVES MORE

PUBLISHED ON FRIDAY 5TH DECEMBER 2014

Tuesday 22nd November - Conference

Bristol Rovers 2   Barnet 1

Taylor - 4', Balanta - 90' +3   Luisma Villa - 37'

Rovers: Mildenhall, Lockyer, McChrystal (Capt.), Parkes, Brown, Della-Verde, Sinclair, Mansell. Monkhouse [Booked] (Harrison – 70'), Blissett (Balanta - 67'), Taylor (Goldberg – 80').

Unused Substitutes: Clarke, Trotman.

Attendance: 6,012 inc 148 Honey Monsters   Referee: Nick Kinseley

Saturday 29th November - Conference

Bristol Rovers 2   Welling United 0

Blissett - 53', Taylor (pen) - 73'

Rovers: Mildenhall, Lockyer, McChrystal (Capt.), [Booked], Parkes, Brown, Monkhouse, Sinclair, Mansell, Gosling (Balanta – 45'), Taylor (Della-Verde – 74'), Wall (Blissett – 45').

Unused Substitutes: Trotman, Goldberg.

Attendance: 5,792 inc 72 Winged Horsemen of the Apocalypse

Referee: Steven Rushton (2nd time this season).

Tuesday 2nd December - Conference

Wrexham 0   Bristol Rovers 0

Rovers: Mildenhall (Trotman – 44'), Lockyer, McChrystal (Capt.), Parkes, Brown, Monkhouse, Sinclair, Mansell, Della-Verde (Balanta – 24'), Taylor [Booked], Blissett [Booked] (Wall – 72').

Unused Substitutes: Clarke, Goldberg.

Attendance: 2,6,08 inc 193 Gas   Referee: Ross Joyce (2nd time this season)

Played 24 Points 42 Position 3rd   *Gap to leaders [Barnet] = 7 points*

Together Everyone Achieves More

Last Saturday a familiar face was spotted walking along the front of the 'Blackthorn' Terrace on his way to do the half time raffle draw as a guest of honour with the Fans Forum Sponsors Club (only £10 to join and amazing benefits to be had). He looked fit and dapper, as befits his post-Rovers career as a fire-fighter, and certainly not a man just into his 50's, so after the tepid first half we had just endured I couldn't resist asking him to nip down the tunnel and get his boots on. Thankfully Darrell Clarke had been watching the same game as me and with a bench bristling full of creativity and attacking intent, and the dullest first XI seen for ages, made two vital changes at half-time that meant Christian McClean wasn't needed after all.

Christian was hardly a Rovers legend in comparison to Big Dev, Boris, Reecy, Ollie, Joner, 20man, Jocky, Scooter et al (everyone had nicknames in those days!), but he was the epitome of a squad player and a professional who would do a job for you. He came to Rovers for a trial in spring 1988 as a 25 year old dominant centre-back from Clacton Town in the Ninth Tier of football, and had never played League football before, but utilised all his stature and physicality to make life uncomfortable for strikers. Gerry Francis decided to make him a gamekeeper turned poacher by converting him into a striker. King Gerry of course had an eye for spotting the most advantageous position on a pitch for each player and for his squad, having already successfully transforming Ian 'Jocky' Alexander from a winger to a full back.

In the next three years Christian was limited to 36 League and Cup starts and 32 sub appearances, including the Leyland DAF Cup-Final at Wembley in 1990, but in the days of only two subs it was actually a very important slot to fill, and although I don't recall him being brought on to sure up the defence I imagine that Gerry had that flexibility in the back of his mind when trusting Christian with the honour of being a loyal replacement. Christian's finest hour, a goal in three consecutive matches in Spring 1990, kept the pressure on League leaders Bristol City, who then faltered at the last hurdle. Those three games were part of the famous run of six 2-1 wins in a row, the last five of which saw Rovers battle back from a goal down each time. Rovers never gave up, and whether it was Big Dev leading the line, or Big Chris, it really didn't matter. We, as fans, knew that our heroes on the pitch would fight to the death for us. And they really did, especially the two goals against Cardiff City in 11 minutes of injury time (yes, that's not a typo, **eleven** minutes!) at Twerton Park in March 1990 to turn a loss into a win. Six weeks later Cardiff were relegated to the bottom division by one solitary point; such are the fine margins of football, and precisely why the lack of fight last season was such a disgrace.

To this day Christian can still recall the lyrics to 'Goodnight Irene', and as Lee Mansell collected his Man of the Match award, Christian gave him a rousing pep talk about how Rovers fans will give you everything they have, and more, and how that bond is irreplaceable.

Football truly is a squad game and as we embark into the F.A. Trophy campaign, and begin to suffer injuries that we had so far avoided, it was the perfect time for one of our most forgotten squad players to revisit the Gas and help remind us of that fact.

We can take many positives from the last 10 days. To beat Barnet in the last minute was exactly the physical and psychological win we needed to keep us within a fighting distance of the Bees, who have led the division since late August. A game of two halves versus Welling showed how a young manager can sometimes get away with a bit of experimentation, even if it fails, and it also handily resulted in both their central midfielders (including their player-manager) being suspended for the oddly timed return visit this Saturday; a rare case of the right team benefiting from the ill discipline of the opposition. Whether or not the laboured looking Alex Wall was deliberately used for only the first half to wear the Welling defenders down, to build his own fitness up, and to give Nathan Blissett a rest, is of course a moot point, but what matters now is that Darrell Clarke did get away with it, and Rovers totally dominated the second half, albeit aided by a sending off.

A point at Wrexham was disappointing in some respects, but having a central defender in goal for 50 minutes and him keeping a clean sheet should never be sniffed at. And at least if we play them again next season (or even in the forthcoming F.A. Trophy competition) we won't need to produce the apocalyptic stats that preceded this meeting; nine defeats on the trot at the Racecourse Ground, the last draw back in 1995, and no win since 1979, although due to the quirks of the fixture list we actually won twice there that year. Even though it was questionable management not to have a goalie on a five man bench, I felt it was at least effective and decisive management to immediately put McChrystal in goal and fill his slot with the most dominant centre back seen at Rovers for many years, Neal Trotman. It was a marriage made in Wales and the shielding defence offered Macca a degree of protection rivalling Offa's Dyke.

To witness the visionary Angelo Balanta now fit and featuring regularly is like rediscovering a player that had been accidentally locked in a broom cupboard for the last two months, and seeing Lyle Della-Verde tie defenders in knots has also brought a smile to Gashead faces. We hope of course that his injury at Wrexham won't be serious. Finally, Bradley Goldberg should provide us with added width options, especially with Della-Verde sidelined, Jake Gosling flitting in and out of the side, and Dave Martin out of favour.

It is very early days for Alex Wall, but his loan signing has meant that Ryan Brunt has been allowed to look elsewhere again, presumably with a view to a move in the near future. Just like Christian McClean became an almost steadfast understudy for Devon White, 'The Wall' may well prove to be an able deputy for Blissett although early sightings of the two clearly suggest Blissett has more of a range of talents, and could well become a season changing signing for us.

GOOD STAT - BAD STAT

Good Stat - Rovers broke the Conference record for the longest ever run without an away loss (20 games from Lincoln City on 13th September 2014 to the FGR Play-Off Semi-Final on 29th April 2015).

Bad Stat - As we were promoted out of the Conference whilst still in that run we could potentially come back and extend it. It's not as deranged a stat as it might sound, as one of the previous joint record holders (Scarborough FC) set the record with their unbeaten away run of 19 matches from 11th October 1986 to 30th August 1999. No, that's not a typo. They were promoted to the Football League in 1987, and relegated back in 1999, and their run spanned the two eras!

WEEK 32 - TO MAKE ONE, THERE MUST BE TWO

PUBLISHED ON FRIDAY 12TH DECEMBER 2014

Saturday 6th December - Conference

Welling United 0   Bristol Rovers 0

Rovers: Spiess, Lockyer, McChrystal (Capt.), Parkes, Sinclair, Clarke [Booked], Mansell, Brown, Balanta (Gosling - 62'), Goldberg (Wall − 62'), Blissett (Taylor −69').

Unused Substitutes: Leadbitter, Trotman.

Attendance: 1,176 inc 651 Gas   Referee: Colin Lymer (2nd time this season)

Played 25 Points 43 Position 2nd   *Gap to leaders [Barnet] = 9 points*

To make one, there must be two

Now that we are just over half the way through the league season it feels the opportune time to take a look forward to the end of the season in May, and also to look back at some of expectations we had in the summer and the decisions we had to make.

After 25 games we have 43 points. Extrapolated across 46 games that would give us 79 points, a total which would have got us into the play-offs only half of the seasons since 2006/7, the year the league first comprised of 24 teams. Of course extrapolating such figures is not completely fair as due to the vagaries of the Conference fixture system we have already completed our fixtures against AFC Telford United, Forest Green Rovers, Wrexham, Barnet and Welling United, but have yet to even sniff Gateshead, Torquay United, or Macclesfield Town, three clubs near the top of the league. This calcula-tion does however give an indicator of what we could expect to achieve based on the results so far.

We therefore may need to gain a few extra points to achieve what seems to now be the minimum expectation (the play-offs), but the strangely better news is that although half of the last eight automatically promoted teams have achieved more than the magical 100 points, on average only 89 points were actually needed.

Although Darrell Clarke has complained about the amount of fixtures we have already played, and I fully accept that as a manager he would have preferred less, I think that overall it could be a blessing in disguise for us as a team, and especially for us fans. Having so many Tuesday evening games (eight so far, including five before the clocks changed) has been lovely for me as a fan, often standing on terraces with just a T-shirt on. Pitches have been excellent and the weather has mainly been kind.

More importantly it means there are no evening games scheduled for the rest of the season, and as the first two rounds of the F.A. Trophy are also on set-aside Saturdays, if we should enjoy a long run in the Trophy (a cup that I personally think we could win) and/or hit bad weather and postponed games, there will be room in the fixture list without too much of a log jam. Last season Cambridge United played a mammoth 60 games whilst on their winding road to winning the Trophy and the play-off final, thus proving that success can breed success. If your squad can cope of course.

Back in mid June I wrote a piece on this weekly blog entitled, "You know we're so very humble", after the incongruous words of Uriah Heep to David Copperfield. I could see a little of BRFC in the obsequiousness of Heep, as in recent years we seemed to have lost some of our humility. But we had a chance to redeem ourselves, and not to expect that so-called little clubs will come to the Mem and lump it up in the air, or treat us with awe.

Rather like a first week in prison, charitable fans of conference teams were quick to educate us on what not to do in our unfamiliar new surroundings. Have these opinions proved true, and how have we got on with the advice?

They advised us not to recruit a team of ex-Football League players, and not to pay said has-beens lots of cash for failure.

I have been consistently pleased that we have really heeded that advice and for the first time in a long while we have a pretty hungry young squad, with a smattering of wise old heads. We can once again hold our heads up high knowing that no-one on the pitch is taking the mickey out of us or coasting along. I can't think of any players who have a questionable mind set or who massively divide opinion on the terraces or on the forums.

We were told not to expect anyone to care who we are or where we've been for the previous 94 years, or for us to imagine teams will see us as their 'Man U' fixture of the season and 'raise their game' against us. Their CLUB may see our large away support as that in financial terms, especially after the loss of Luton fanatics, but the eleven on the pitch certainly won't.

Well, I'm not quite so sure on this one. Of course it is hard to quantify exactly, and rather subjective, but I feel that some of the smaller teams in particular may have been rather lifted by the prospect of putting one over on a full-time team who arrive with lots of away fans, especially when some of those fans, whilst generally being supportive, can become hugely frustrated at where we are in the football pyramid and why we can't beat such teams. I don't think opponents have raised themselves at our home matches though; indeed, I would suggest that teams like Nuneaton were actually slightly overawed by playing at a bigger stadium and in front of a large crowd. We ourselves sadly seem to hold firm to a historical Apartheid though; one of the few things I dislike about our manager is when he remarks that our opponent is an ex-League team and will thus be very tough to play against.

We were told to expect good quality, fast, and raw, attacking football.

Again the jury is out on this one. We've certainly not seen many teams really attack at the Mem, and no away team has scored more than one goal here. As we have climbed the table away teams seem to have become more defensive towards us. Although there is some pace and skill in the league, many players have clearly shown a first touch or a finishing prowess that explains why they are playing in non-league. Barn doors and banjos have often been mentioned around me on the terraces. It seems like the most eye catching players get hoovered up very quickly by League teams, sometimes before we even get to see them in action against us, as already demonstrated in the case of Harry Beautyman at Welling United. And both Chey Dunkley and Nathan Blissett played their final games for Kidderminster Harriers at the Mem, before being snapped up by Oxford United and us, respectively.

I've not yet seen a team to fear in this league. Even Barnet were a vastly different prospect at the Mem compared to when we faced them at the Hive, although it would be fair to say the difference was at least partly through our team getting much stronger and assured in the intervening three months, and it being a game that Barnet only really needed to draw. In fact I would say it was us who 'raised our game' against them, which shows that this isn't a phenomenon that can to be denied at any level of football, or any team.

Our defence is the second most miserly in the division. If we can just release the brakes a little, and secure some more attacking options in midfield and down the sides (from front to back) I think we could give the Bees a real run for their honey in the second half of the season.

WEEK 33 - A MATTER OF PERSPECTIVE

PUBLISHED ON WEDNESDAY 17TH DECEMBER 2014

Saturday 13th December - FA Trophy 1st Round

Bristol Rovers 0   **Bath City 2**

Own Goal - 68', Artus - 71'

Rovers: Spiess, Leadbitter, Trotman (Capt.), Parkes, Brown, Balanta, Clarke, Sinclair, Martin (Gosling - 62'), Taylor (Goldberg - 73'), Blissett (Wall - 45').

Unused Substitutes: McChrystal, Harrison.

Attendance: 3,505 inc 404 Romans   Referee: Adam Hopkins

A Matter of Perspective

Saturday's game against Bath City was beautifully described as a fragment of a 'special relationship' between our two clubs, rather then the usual 'special rivalry' chestnut.

At the risk of sounding shamelessly self promoting, I feel that one of the more succinct contributions to the book I have recently released (256 pages of pure Gas for only a tenner; available from *www.awaythegas.org.uk*, the club shop at the Mem and the Supporters Club shop on Two Mile Hill - end of advert) actually sums up my own feelings so admirably that it is worth reproducing verbatim.

"When Home is Away by FabGas -

One of my best away day memories was actually when we played Bath City in the F.A. Cup First Round at Twerton Park in November 1994. As we were officially the away team some Gas supporters went into the away end, but with almost 7,000 there Gasheads were spread out everywhere. Some, like myself, stood in the same place as usual, often finding a Bath City fan or two in 'their' space."

"We crushed our hosts 5-0, with Paul Miller bagging four, and Vaughan Jones on the 'wrong' side, but that was almost not as important as the whole experience, which was possibly unique and will probably never happen again. It was all good natured and proved that it is possible to have a match where all fans can behave without the need for segregation (like those rugger fans manage to do every match)."

Lovers of 'Bovver' will perhaps roll their eyes at such sentimental claptrap, but whilst I do like a bit of a bite to a match, and a smattering of caustic banter between fans, I feel that modern life is already hostile enough without adding football violence and blood boiling hatred into the mix.

I don't know if it crossed our clubs mind to consider advertising the match as un-segregated but I wish they had. It would have been a lovely touch, and for once would have got our fans some positive press coverage. Many Gasheads hold a special place in their heart for Bath City, with great memories of their offer to host us for what turned out to be ten long years of exile at Twerton Park, and I can't imagine any trouble would have occurred. I know I am not alone amongst Rovers fans by trying to see the Romans play once or twice each season, if only just to stand on the same terrace that we used to bounce up and down on, and to unearth a cup of tea for only 60p.

A lot of non-league games are un-segregated, and apparently we are a non-league team now. Judging from the boos and negative chants at the end of the match it seems like some Gasheads may need reminding of that fact. Losing to Bath City really isn't the end of the world, and although some may accuse me of having low standards, I would answer that a more prosaic response to Saturday's defeat is not about lowering expectations, it's about keeping your powder dry for a game that really matters. If we are still fighting for promotion in April and we lose our last two home games to Southport and Alfreton, then I will be more tempted to get myself worked up.

Bath City are only one level down from us at the moment, and merely provided us with a dose of our own medicine. How many times have we been to a cup tie, provided most of the atmosphere, got ourselves and our team 'up for a shock', and then provided it? Then we invariably rubbed the home fans noses in it and they ran off to the local media calling for the head of their manager. In return we considered them to be conceited and disrespectful of our efforts, whilst we ourselves took our eye off the ball and would lose our next league game.

On Saturday the reverse happened. And it will continue happening in cup matches until the world gulps its final breath.

Yes, it was an awful performance. Yes, we lost. Yes, it was the first time an away team had scored twice at the Mem this season. But I'm not going to start singing 'what a load of rubbish', especially to a team that was significantly weaker than our best starting XI. I just fail to see how that helps. It is blindingly obvious to everyone that it was a very poor performance from us, and a decent, committed performance from the Romans. As Arnold Beisser wrote, "the tragic or the humorous is a matter of perspective".

There are only two good times to depart this competition; at Wembley, or in the First Round. This isn't the F.A. Cup or the League Cup. There is zero chance of a 'big game' until five punishing rounds later, in North London, and even then it would most probably be a smaller payday than drawing an away tie at a top Premier League team.

The important lesson to learn whenever tempted to play a weakened team again is that it wasn't just the personnel changes themselves that made a real difference, but also the fact that Trotman, Leadbitter, Clarke, Wall, Gosling and Martin have played very few games in the last two months and looked rusty, and perhaps even more importantly have not been playing regularly TOGETHER, unlike our best team has.

FAN CONTRIBUTIONS NEEDED

'Twerton Delight: Full of Eastern Promise'

My next book will be similar to 'Away The Gas', but the subject is the amazing decade we spent at Twerton from 1986 to 1996.

Get writing and don't keep those memories and photos only to yourself; share them with your fellow Gasheads and become a published writer at the same time. See page 74 for more details.

WEEK 34 - THE MEASURE OF INTELLIGENCE IS THE ABILITY TO CHANGE

PUBLISHED ON WEDNESDAY 24TH DECEMBER 2014

Friday 19th December - Conference

Bristol Rovers 3	Gateshead 2
Clarke - 59', Mansell - 69', Sinclair - 72'	Pattison - 18', Rodman - 62'

Rovers: Spiess, Lockyer, McChrystal (Capt.) (Trotman - 66'), Parkes, Sinclair, Mansell [Booked], Brown, Monkhouse, Balanta (Clarke - 29'), Taylor, Wall (Harrison - 85').

Unused Substitutes: Gosling, Goldberg.

Attendance: 5,367 inc 46 Heeds on a ridiculously long Friday night trip.

Referee: Brett Huxtable (3rd time this season, and already three times too many)

Played 26 Points 46 Position 2nd   *Gap to leaders [Barnet] = 9 points*

The measure of intelligence is the ability to change

If Barnet manager Martin Allen considered Rovers fans 'rambunctious' whilst playing our best football this season and narrowing beating his table topping team last month, I doubt he would be able to find a superior superlative in the dictionary for Friday's 3-2 win against Gateshead when we were mediocre at times but showed astonishing fight to come back from behind twice.

At half-time the natives were restless, not just because we were one down, but because Gateshead had a clear and effective game plan, whilst we misplaced passes and showed skill levels and confidence on the ball that were far below those from the Heed.

Their opening goal just about summed it up. A 60 metre cross field ball from a right back was taken down on a sixpence and opened up our right hand side who were already struggling due to the worst performance so far from Angelo Balanta (hauled off after 29 minutes, possibly injured) and still having a centre back playing at right back. Not that long after the ball was in the net. 'Ultra long ball and grab' may be a new phrase I have just invented, but it worked well and was not just kick and rush.

I have been a Basketball fan since becoming friends with Tony Brown, a retired semi-pro, 15 years ago. Basketball has a Ronseal entitled tactic called a 'full court press' where instead of the usual policy of defending in your own half and allowing the opposition to get to the half way line before getting in their faces, you press them in both halves. As basketball is a game for only five players this leads to five one-on-one battles which can be exhilarating, but creates huge spaces on the court, and is often only used towards the end of a game, and by a team losing and desperate to force the issue, to fatigue the opposition and to save some clock time.

Rovers were faced with the same dilemma, but in this situation the decision was needed right from the start of the game. As Gateshead confidently passed it around the back five waiting for spaces and opportunities to appear Rovers had to either press them high up the pitch, or accept that we would rarely acquire any possession, and as they say, you can't score without the ball. The crowd of course wanted the former, and to be blunt it was dull to watch for a considerable while.

Bringing on Ollie Clarke for Balanta and switching The Beard to a more advanced role was a master stroke and gave more bite to our midfield, in a game patrolled by a ref who never whistles (more on him later). Full credit should be given to Darrell Clarke, who has not been afraid to make several early changes this season, something that Albert Einstein would have been proud of. We may not have the best players in the league, and seemingly not the best coaches, but we have the best adaptable tactician at the helm. The concern though is why we didn't counter Gateshead right from when we announced our line-up, as presumably we had done our due diligence on their style of play?

The following is hardly a spectacular revelation, but Conference Premier football, nay football of most levels, seems to be as much about who makes the least mistakes as to who is positively excelling.

Individual errors made a huge contribution to their goals, the first brace for a league team at the Mem this season. The first saw Mark McChrystal play everyone onside and then fail to clear a ball that deflected across the box, leaving Matty Pattison to slide in behind him (not helped by Tom Lockyer being the wrong side of his man, the scorer). Their second saw Ollie Clarke dispossessed in midfield, and Lockyer allowing himself to unnecessarily get sucked into the centre, whilst Alex Rodman galloped up to the left hand side of the penalty area, exactly where a right back should be.

Having said this, all of the five goals also showed some considerable individual skill. Lee Mansell is a genuinely top class free kick taker and Ollie Clarke has been a long range shooting sensation this season. The weakest part of Stuart Sinclair's game is his goal scoring, and it still will be next game as he has failed to put away several chances this season, but his left footed blaster when two defenders were covering their errant goalie was a fabulous net buster to top yet another heroic Man of the Match performance. On the other side veteran John Oster will be disappointed to pick up two goal assists from his threatening cross balls yet still come home empty handed, and their attackers in general can be proud of their considerable skills.

However, for all of Gateshead's swagger and admirable football, all three teams in recent history who tried to play it about the back five at the Mem left with plaudits but no points (Barnet losing 2-1 in February 2013 and Nuneaton failing 3-1 in September this season). The lesson seems to be that penetration is more important than pure possession.

Referee Brett Huxtable must live in Southmead and only ask for a couple of pasties as payment as we were also allocated him for FC Halifax Town in August and Kidderminster Harriers in November. His performances are certainly remarkably consistent. Consistently terrible, with a comedic routine more akin to Cliff Huxtable from 'The Cosby Show', and the fitness of an asthmatic snail. I suspect he may have been a warder at Guantanamo Bay in a previous life as you'd need to have your leg severed into two burnt portions by a bolt of lightning for him blow his whistle.

Whilst I appreciate a ref who allows the game to flow, I don't appreciate a ref who won't even allow a physio onto a pitch when Mark McChrystal stayed down after a head-on collision with his own keeper, and was very clearly seriously hurt, all whilst the ball had naturally gone out of play minutes before. Thirty years ago the prompt actions of Rovers' physio Roy Dolling helped save the lives of both Aiden McCaffrey (at Southend United in April 1984) and Ian Alexander (Fisher Athletic in November 1988) when they 'swallowed' their tongue / dentures, respectively. It seems like the Conference have learnt little in the intervening decades.

We all know the quality of the officials at this level is appalling, but then again we are in the Fifth Tier, so we are getting officials that are even worse than anything we've ever experienced before. Mr Huxtable never gives anything so you might as well get used to it, and you might as well tell your players to get stuck in when he is in the middle. We did that in the second half and even the normally level headed Lee Mansell almost lost his rag before turning a would-be Glasgow kiss into a Bristol bromance.

Although our home form is great we must still work on our away performances, as amongst our 10 remaining away games we are playing the entire current top eight teams, except Barnet. We haven't lost at Plainmoor since 2003 (a five game streak), and what price another piece of Mansell magic, back at a club where he is sixth on their all-time appearance list?

WEEK 35 - IF YOU WANT TO GET AHEAD, FOLLOW THE HATTERS

PUBLISHED ON WEDNESDAY 31ST DECEMBER 2014

Friday 26th December - Conference

Torquay United 1   **Bristol Rovers 2**

Spiess (o.g.) - 34'   Taylor - 8', Trotman - 31'

Rovers: Spiess, Leadbitter, Trotman, Parkes, Lockyer, Mansell (Capt.), Monkhouse, Gosling, Sinclair, Taylor (Goldberg - 90'), Blissett [Booked] (Wall - 66').

Unused Substitutes: Puddy, Martin, Harrison.

Attendance: 3,755 inc 1,145 Gas.   Referee: Adam Bromley (2nd time this season)

Sunday 28th December - Conference

Bristol Rovers 4   **Macclesfield Town 0**

Monkhouse - 44', Blissett - 65',
Taylor - 76', Harrison (pen) - 83'

Rovers: Puddy, Leadbitter, McChrystal (Capt.), Parkes, Lockyer, Gosling (Clarke - 64'), Mansell, Sinclair, Monkhouse, Taylor (Goldberg - 79'), Blissett (Harrison - 79').

Unused Substitutes: Spiess, Trotman.

Attendance: 6,943 inc 140 Silkmen.   Referee: Rob Whitton (2nd time this season)

Played 28 Points 52 Position 2nd   *Gap to leaders [Barnet] = 7 points*

If you want to get ahead, follow the Hatters

It comes as a minor relief to Gasheads to be going into a New Year whilst second in a football table, even if it is at the lowest level of football we have faced since joining the Football League in 1920. We may have many minor gripes about the season so far, but the table tells a decent story, and it is the first time since 2009 that we are even in the top half of the table at the end of a calendar year.

In nine dreadful seasons in League Two we were time and again no-where near the top half of the table on New Year's Eve; our average position in fact being a dismal 17th. I could never see how we could be promoted if we didn't get into the top half of the division. Being in or near the top twelve by New Year at least gives you some chance of pushing up and into the play-offs (like in 2006/7), or in the case of League Two, the only division where four go up, maybe even into the automatic promotion places. The fact that in those nine seasons we only had one play-off slot, and even that came on the last day of the season, courteous of an unexpected and late win against the table toppers, Hartlepool United, was a lasting disgrace to our club and our loyal supporters. We only finished in the top half of the table two other times and they were both 12th.

Thankfully we can finally enjoy a Christmas period as we continue to cement a play-off place and keep within a reasonable distance of runaway leaders Barnet in the hope they may slip up, or that we can at least chip away at a lead that has now been slightly reduced to seven points.

Another 1,000+ following of ever dependable Gasheads made the Boxing Day trip to the English Riviera, and were rewarded with a win that was apparently comfortable in the main, but in typical Rovers style left fans heavy breathing until the final bell.

On Sunday we dismantled a really pitiable Macclesfield Town team and registered our first three goal (or more) win of the league season. I appreciate that every team has an off day now and again, and having a paltry three subs on the bench tells its own tale of the injuries they must have, but on that performance it seems quite shocking that the Silkmen are third in this league, and you could certainly see why they have scored the least goals amongst the top 12 teams.

It has been encouraging that many fringe or previously injured players were reported to have had a good game at Plainmoor, and I saw some proficient performances myself against Macclesfield Town. Before this week some fans seemed to have given up on Daniel Leadbitter, as his defensive abilities are weak, but I have always seen an exciting footballer in there; we just need to work out where and when to use him effectively. It's great to hear that Neal Trotman is back to his dominant best, whilst Tom Parkes has quietly been winning plaudits for several months now. To have three centre backs of the quality of Macca, Parkesy and Trotters is reassuring as we go into our final 18 games with the best ranked defence in the League. Jake Gosling has struggled to make much impact until now, but he was some people's Man of the Match on Friday, finding the space of an away game and the heavy conditions to his liking, and was excellent on Sunday as well. Nathan Blissett sorely needed a goal after a few close range misses, so being positioned where all good poachers operate (namely the six yard line) to slot home Monkhouse's cut back could be a really important moment for our new signing, who after all is still a young lad tentatively finding his way. Tom Lockyer has coped well at left back, and although Andy Monkhouse is certainly not your conventional winger, he adds height and a goal scoring threat to our team. Indeed our team for the last few games must have been the tallest team we've had for a long time, with Leadbitter and Monkhouse adding a threat few teams can boast in those positions.

Although our current form is good we will still have to work on our away performances as amongst our nine remaining away games we are playing the entire current top eight teams, except Barnet and Eastleigh. We shouldn't be totally disheartened by this tough task though, as overall most teams have hard games to come. Barnet have 10 games left against top 12 teams, whereas we have nine. Macclesfield have nine as well (but seven of them are away), Grimsby Town have nine (six of which are against the top five teams), and Eastleigh have 13 such games left and so far have only registered one win against a top 12 side in nine attempts.

The following may sound slightly ambitious but I feel we need to target a win at EVERY home game until the end of the season to stand a chance of automatic promotion. We only have three of the current top 12 left to play at home (Eastleigh, Torquay United and Lincoln City), with six the bottom 12 still to come. Whilst I'm not suggesting we are anywhere near as good as Luton Town last season, they certainly showed how to flat track bully the lower teams, dropping only a brace of points at home against the bottom 12 clubs, and rattling in 37 goals to only a handful conceded.

It's easy to forget but we did actually dispatch the lower teams at home last season quite well, picking up 22 points at home to the bottom half teams, out of a possible 33 on offer.

Having already opened Pandora's box by mentioning last seasons' eventual runaway Champions Luton Town, I may as well go the whole hog and recall that they didn't actually hit the top of the table until their biggest home win of the season to that point in time, on, yes, you guessed it, the 28th of December, which had followed a 2-1 away win on Boxing Day! Both teams also had poor starts to the season and neither hit the Top 10 until exactly their tenth game.

Co-incidence or fate? You decide. I'm off to stick pins in my John Akinde doll.

WEEK 36 - TURKEY OF THE YEAR AWARD

PUBLISHED ON WEDNESDAY 7TH JANUARY 2015

Thursday 1st January - Conference

Bristol Rovers 1   Torquay United 1

Taylor (pen) - 83'   Ofori-Acheampong - 10'

Rovers: Puddy, Leadbitter, Trotman (McChrystal - 48'), Parkes, Lockyer, Sinclair, Mansell (Capt.), Clarke (Gosling - 63'), Monkhouse, Taylor Blissett (Harrison - 74').

Unused Substitutes: Spiess, Goldberg.

Attendance: 8,206 inc 424 Gulls.   Referee: Simon Bennett (2nd time this season)

Sunday 4 th January - Conference

Nuneaton Town 0   Bristol Rovers 2

Mansell - 40', Blissett - 49'

Rovers: Puddy, Lockyer, McChrystal (Capt.), Parkes, Brown, Gosling, Sinclair, Mansell (Clarke - 90'), Monkhouse, Taylor (Goldberg - 80'), Blissett (Harrison - 87').

Unused Substitutes: Leadbitter, Balanta.

Attendance: 1,661 inc 976 Gas.   Referee: Jason Whiteley

Played 30 Points 56 Position 2nd   *Gap to leaders [Barnet] = 6 points*

Turkey of the Year Award

If Rovers get into the play-offs by a point, or even win the league by that little digit, we might wish to send a Methuselah of Champagne to Torquay United's foolish centre back Angus MacDonald.

I have admittedly missed three home games, but the Gulls (or should that be the Turkeys?) were the best team I've seen at the Mem this season, until they allowed us to grab a barely deserved point courtesy of a few moments of madness.

Torquay are of course a bit of a bogey team for us at the Mem, and were the perfect banana skin after a heavy night out. We may not have lost at Plainmoor since 2003 (a run of six matches) but most Gasheads will painfully recall the 2-1 loss last season in a crucial April game, with the Gulls 11 points below us in the table, on a roll of four straight losses, and having returned pointless from 14 of their 20 away games. It was only our fifth home loss of the season but that was the match that really got fans worrying. Shaquile Coulthirst's opener was their club's first goal in 420 minutes of football, and a certain Lee Mansell bagged the crucial second.

And how can we forget Paul Buckle's first home game in charge, in August 2011, a quirk of timing that proved we had somehow upset the fixture Gods. Buckle had left the Gulls with indecent haste a mere two days after his side lost in the play-off final, so a packed away end displaying a huge homemade banner reading 'Judas' came as no complete surprise, amidst mutterings that his sizeable head had already been turned before that final. Buckle had also returned to raid his former employers of Scott Bevan and top scorer Chris Zebroski, although he probably should have actually brought Euan O'Kane and Lee Mansell with him instead. The ranks of Gasheads in the bumper 8,427 crowd had patently forgot what happened after our previous relegation to League Two in 2001, and we were two down within 15 sun baked minutes. After this unsurprising demise Buckle made the first of several interview gaffs by telling Radio Bristol that, "We didn't see that coming."

Returning to the present day, the seasiders possessed a rare combination of height, power AND pace up front, in Ryan Bowman and Duane Ofori-Acheam-pong, plus a decent understanding of each other to boot. Winger Jordan Chapell also impressed, and overall they were a team that both physically and mentally belied the dominant away defeat we had inflicted on them barely six days previously.

Yet in the 71st minute MacDonald managed to acquire himself only the second booking of the contest from a referee who, like most others in the Conference, usually has cobwebs in his top pocket. Only 11 minutes later the referee's assistant seemed to spot some relatively minor obstruction in the penalty area by MacDonald on Ellis Harrison and after a brief talk to the referee a penalty was awarded, to much hilarity from the Blackthorn Terrace. The Gulls obviously swooped on the officials like a chip-stealing flock of *Larus argentatus* and the way that Ofori-Acheampong got up-close and personal with them gave the ref little option but to book the big fella. Maybe it was a deliberate smokescreen to take the heat off of MacDonald? If so, MacDonald wasn't cool enough to grasp the lifeline he was offered, inexplicably remain-ing in the danger zone until the ref pulled out a second yellow to give him his fourth red card of an infinitesimal career, and finally silence his loose tongue.

Interestingly it still doesn't seem clear what the penalty and booking were actually given for though as the referee's assistant patently made a little nodded head gesture which suggested he also informed the ref of a modest tête-à-tête that MacDonald and Harrison shared after the foul in question.

As MacDonald trudged off he even gave Harrison another bite and a terrifying lingering pointy finger, as if he still didn't comprehend that he had given us a point on a plate, plus a decent chance of pressing a 10 man team for a winner. Maybe their lack of discipline should come as no surprise given the example they are offered by boss Chris Hargreaves, a serial whinger who labelled the decision 'disgraceful', and earlier in the season claimed that in another year none of Ofori-Acheampong's five yellow cards collected before the end of September would have been awarded. He is currently on nine yellows, the same as MacDonald and 21 yr old captain Luke Young. I assume that for the rest of the season Hargreaves will be wearing a 'Why always us?' T-shirt, hand scrawled in crayon as if made by a Broadmoor patient.

As Jimmy Greaves used to say on 'Saint and Greavsie', "football is a funny old game". It seems hard to explain how we can give the third placed team (Macclesfield Town) a total thrashing and get rather excited at reducing the gap to Barnet to seven points, and then four days later see nothing go right, with misplaced passes, scuffed shots and possession rapidly turned over as if the ball was in fact a large baked potato. We made it look like we were playing the Eagles, the Canaries or the Throstles, rather than the humble dive-bombing, faecal fixated Gulls.

That well taken penalty kept Barnet's lead down to a mere nine points, which sounds so much better than a psychologically damaging double digit figure, and our doggedness was rewarded on Sunday when a perfect set of results cut it to an appetising six points.

With a fortnight for rest and rumination, I know which set of players I would prefer to be within right now. The atmosphere in our camp must be electric, whereas for Barnet it has always been their Championship to lose. Although they are clearly a very good team, they have never gone more than six games without a defeat, whereas we have had a run of nine undefeated, and are currently in a run of 13. Both of us have tough away games next, but we are very fortunate to be facing a previously excellent Woking side now in free fall, having gained just two points from their last six games.

WEEK 37 - RUSH GOALIE

PUBLISHED ON WEDNESDAY 14TH JANUARY 2015

No recent results as it was an FA Trophy weekend. We were left without a game, as were Barnet, so we remained 6 points behind them.

One of the best, and simultaneously worst, aspects of Rovers being in the Football League was getting a cursory one minute slot every Saturday on BBC1's 'The Football League Show'. The down side was that it would probably be 1am by the time the Pirates were on, and that was after being forced to listen to the dullsville middle of the road remarks of Leroy ("when I was at Torquay..." - that three and a half years now feels like it lasted longer than Alex Ferguson at Man U) Rosenior or the nasal whine of Steve Claridge.

Many years ago in the nascent days of the media finally cottoning onto the excitement, colour and skill of the Africa Cup of Nations, I got up early on a Sunday to watch a live match they were showing on some sort of cable channel or early red button invention. Given that about 12 men and a dog were probably watching, the commentator was straight out of a media studies course and the summariser was Steve Claridge, in his very early days away from the smell of liniment in his day job. They encouraged the said 'crowd' of viewers to send questions in, so I crank started my brick shaped mobile phone and rattled off a question somewhere along the lines of, 'Are you going to do any analysis of the game, or just describe things we can see with our own eyes?'. It miraculously got ticker taped along the bottom of the screen, and I was honoured to be on the end of a Claridge rant and the immortal bleat of, 'what side of the bed did he get out of this morning?'.

In June this year it finally dawned on me that our relegation had so many knock-on effects. We obviously weren't even a 'League' club anymore, so we wouldn't be on the Football League Show, wouldn't be in the League Cup, wouldn't be in the Johnstone's Paint Trophy, and to rub it in even more, not only would any away matches I go to not count towards my long-term quest of seeing a game at all of the 92 League clubs, but that suddenly one of the 66 clubs I had visited (my own club!), could no longer even be counted on my list. Thankfully this myriad of negatives were all neatly balanced by being on TV more than ever before, even if it was only BT Sport, and having a newspaper dedicated to us; the Non-League Football Paper. Muh.

Not surprisingly I stopped bothering to even tune in to the Football League Show.

Something however drew me back last Saturday evening, as if fate was willing me to witness the uproarious sight of ex-Rovers striker Matt Harrold donning a goalkeeping jersey for Crawley Town when regular keeper Brian Jensen was injured with over 50 minutes still to play. With no sub goalie the ginger ninja was apparently picked to put on the absurdly over padded gloves because he is somewhat lanky, rather than due to any previous experience, or feline like cameos and scorpion kicks in training.

The fact that MK Dons put two past him to salvage a draw, and that 2-2 was still considered a good result by Crawley fans and worthy of a MOTM award for 'the cat', puts **Mark McChrystal**'s clean sheet against Wrexham a month ago into startling perspective.

Seeing a grown man hurriedly pulling on a padded jersey three sizes too big for him, then forget the gloves, whilst proceeding to try to look professional in a job he's most probably never done before is one of the rare joys of being a football fan, but one that had been getting rarer each year since the 1993/94 season, when three subs were first allowed and goalies regularly featured on benches. Although various league and cup competitions now customarily allow five subs to be named, sometimes even seven, the pressure to make crucial creative substitutions that can flip a game on its head, coupled with the modern day absence of true utility men, has somewhat counter intuitively resulted in more Harrold / McChrystal moments of late, as five outfield players preen themselves on the sidelines, waiting to be the feted game changer. Maybe it's time for 'rush goalie' to finally be added to the rule book?

What Rovers fan of a certain age can ever forget **David Mehew** temporarily going in goal at Trashton on New Years Day 1987 to replace Timmy Carter for about 15 minutes whilst he recovered from the battering of shots that had rained down on him from a dominant Robins side. If it was a boxing match it would have been stopped, but Boris and Timmy kept a clean sheet between them and over 17,000 hung over souls could hardly believe their bleary eyes when a last minute sucker punch from Gary Smart won the game for the brave boys in blue.

Bob Bloomer, the classic utility man and hardly blessed with the stature of a Nigel Martyn or the presence of a Kevin Miller, also deserves a special mention for going in goal when Brian Parkin was injured in an FA Cup match against Crewe Alexandra in January 1991. Losing 2-0 at home may not sound so bad today, but as the Railwaymen were a division below and in the relegation zone at the time, it was a mini-disaster during Gerry Francis's final year as our mercurial manager.

When Mr.Glum was sent off against Brighton two months later it was **Ian 'Jocky' Alexander**'s turn to go between the sticks. When his first touch was to save the resulting penalty from John Byrne he was bestowed with instant hero status, as if chopping down numerous City wingers wasn't already enough to give him a place in the Rovers 'Hall of Fame'. No-one now of course remembers, nor cares, that we lost 3-1.

Returning to the present day, we regularly walk the sub goalie tightrope, although Steve Mildenhall will apparently be back soon.

With a two week break, two new signings, and more rest to come due to the farcical forced postponement of our next home game for the sake of the FA Trophy, we enter into this final push with the strongest and fittest squad we've had all season, and a genuine chance to remind Barnet that their rivals are not just going to stand and watch them march to the title.

There is little I can really add to the recent coming and goings at the Mem. I doubt anyone could argue with Fabien Spiess, Dave Martin and Alex Wall all departing (with our best wishes) after disappointing loan spells, nor on the other hand the exciting arrival of number one target Jermaine Easter. Matt Tubbs would have been just as agreeable, and at three years younger a signing with a longer future, but Portsmouth have a tedious reputation for big spending and little success, so if he prefers to be there then he's not quite the right player for us. We now have a player who was held in high regard at Millwall and it's difficult to find a bad word said about his attitude and professionalism, which I imagine is precisely why Darrell Clarke has wanted him for several months now.

WEEK 38 - IT WAS ON THE CARDS

PUBLISHED ON TUESDAY 20TH JANUARY 2015

Saturday 17th January - Conference

Woking 0   Bristol Rovers 0

Rovers: Puddy, Lockyer, McChrystal (Capt.), Parkes, Brown, Gosling, Mansell, Clarke [Booked] (Leadbitter), Monkhouse, Taylor (Harrison - 75'), Blissett (Easter - 58').

Unused Substitutes: Mildenhall, Dawson.

Attendance: 3,853 inc at least 1,869 Gas.   Referee: David Rock

Played 31 Points 57 Position 2nd   *Gap to leaders [Barnet] = 5 points*

It was on the cards

Occasionally you will hear a football fan saying 'that was the best 0-0 I've seen for ages'. Sadly that phrase wasn't used by any of 1,869 Gasheads who were officially counted at Woking on Saturday (nor others who were unofficially in other parts of the ground). This game really was an old fashioned nil-nil dullfest, and both teams were lucky to even get nil. Sadly the atmosphere was also dead as a dodo, not helped by two-thirds of the Gasheads being strung out along the long, thin terrace, whilst the 600 others were away in the seats at the far end.

A point is a point, but there was a tinge of disappointment at the result after seeing Barnet lose again away from home, although that defeat was at a tough club that we ourselves will be visiting on Valentine's Day [Grimsby Town]. If we had been offered a point a month or more ago I suspect most of us would have been happy to take it, but after the Cards had a December slump our expectations had risen.

On the pitch it was a woefully turgid game and rather made a mockery of the idea that a two week break would do us good, whereas part-time Woking would undoubtedly wane after tackling two FA Trophy matches during our fallow period. It was actually Rovers who looked languid and rusty, whilst Woking looked as sharp as a fresh deck of cards. Neither team however showed the quality needed to break down the resolute defences whose proficiency cancelled each other out. It might as well have been a game between two bowling machines borrowed from the local cricket club; spitting out balls for the four excellent centre halves to deal with.

The obligatory 'guy behind me on the terrace' was spot on when he raised the question cum statement of "why all this 'ball over the top' nonsense?!". We don't normally play that way and as the first XI hadn't really changed since that successful festive period (just Ollie Clarke in for an injured Beard), it seemed baffling why we thought that Blissett and Taylor had overnight become the reincarnation of Roberts and Cureton from the late 1990's.

At least we can be delighted to see Macca back to his best, and what he lacks in pace he makes up with positioning and experience. Tom Parkes gets better every game and his confidence on the ball, his little tricks, and even his passing has improved exponentially. His solidity is now almost taken for granted and if any of the rumours are true about League teams looking to bid for him, then we need to realise that he is the one member of the defence we really cannot afford to lose as he is our lynchpin, and having turned 23 last week he still has a decade or more in him, unlike Trotman and Macca.

There must be a defensive fetish in the Woking area as the only notable relationship we previously had with the Cardinals was paying a whopping £150,000 for the impressive centre back Steve Foster in May 1997 after his solitary season for the Cards during their golden period - between 1994 and 1997 they finishing runners-up in the Conference twice and won the FA Trophy three times.

Players who have appeared for both sides include Scott Rendell (a noteworthy striker), Elvis Hammond (surely the only ex-Pirate with a middle name of Zark) and Jefferson Louis, but then again Mr Louis has played for 92.7% of all non-league teams in the UK (fact... maybe). This deadly trio shared between them a staggering... nil goals in the blue and white quarters. Later, in 2012, Hammond was all shock up when sentenced to a year at Her Majesty's pleasure for his part in a money laundering operation, but at least he did make the jailhouse rock whilst inside. On his release he joined Farnborough and when their squad was re-branded in a bizarre sponsorship deal each player was given the name of a famous footballer to officially adopt and wear on their shirt. Hammond, quite inexplicably, got 'Pele'!

There was more drama off the pitch than on it, with several hundred Pirates locked out of the ground after the peculiar sounding away figure of 1,869 was reached. It was an invasion of the likes not seen since the aliens landed at nearby Horsell Common in H.G. Wells' 'The War of the Worlds'. Some observers bizarrely held the fans themselves responsible or even BRFC. As the blame game has since unfurled it is hard to know quite who to believe, but the bottom line is that it is Woking's ground, not ours, and Surrey Police's patch, not Avon & Somerset's, and for travelling away fans to be locked out of any ground that holds 6,000 yet only had 3,853 actually in it is a complete farce in anyone's language.

The fixture was the perfect storm for us fans and they had been warned, yet failed to adequately provide for us. It was an easy car journey, yet also well served by a busy train station within a suitable walk. Woking is near enough to London and the South-East to attract our numerous fans exiled there and with no game for two weeks before or two weeks after, two new signings to hopefully get a glimpse of, a gap of over five weeks between any games at the Mem, and the Gas on a roll (including winning our last two away games) they really should have thought about this a bit more.

They can't have their cake and eat it can they? Why was there an absurd over abundance of Police if they hadn't expected a huge following, and surely you can't decide to segregate a match but then also continue the quaint non-league custom of 'swapping ends' at half time, as many from the Kingsfield Road Terrace (behind the goal) went to stand in the far corner for the second half, the beautifully entitled 'Moaner's Corner'. Anyway, why this siege mentality in the first place? We've never even played each other before, and there is certainly no beef between the clubs or fans; more likely a collective ignorance of one another. Why couldn't they just treat it as a nice little pay day, and a good sing song between friendly fans. Sadly, if this travesty of a mockery of a sham of a mockery had finished in 'trouble' it would have been splashed all over the media, whereas headlines such as 2,000+ Gasheads behave well, with several hundred inexplicably locked out, don't sell papers do they?

Barnet's lead on us is coming down, and their first back-to-back losses of the season may prove notable, but it's hardly a two horse race. Whilst I don't feel the pack behind us will all win their games in hand, when everything is equal the top five could be a very replete clique indeed.

WEEK 39 – BE GOOD TO YOURSELF, AND EVEN BETTER TO OTHERS

PUBLISHED ON TUESDAY 27TH JANUARY 2015

No recent results as it was an FA Trophy weekend and with Braintree Town still in the competition our scheduled match with them had to be postponed until 24th February. Barnet played and won, so we were now eight points behind them, but with a game in hand. We also dropped to third, behind Macclesfield Town, but only on goals scored.

With yet another barren weekend Rovers fans embarked on a multitude of alternatives last Saturday, from putting up shelves to watching our old friends Bath City continue their impressive march in the F.A. Trophy.

One thing most of us probably weren't doing though was sitting down with a rosy red pen to write a Valentine's card to the head cheese of J. Sainsbury plc.

It comes as no surprise that the BRFC Board of Directors have felt they need to take Sainsbury's to the High Court as it has seemed clear for quite some time that behind the scenes the behemoth retailer has been having cold feet about agreeing to buy the land owned by Rovers in Horfield, and that their wallet really isn't in this love affair.

If this was an episode of Eastenders I suspect the obligatory relationship blow-up scene would have been played out by now and the bling engage-ment ring would have been ripped off in a fit of pique and sinking like a stone to the bottom of the River Avon.

Usually it is us fans and Rovers who resemble a miss matched couple, aptly described after the shocking relegation in May by David Roberts in my recent book as, "a one-sided love affair, unrequited love, but only one of us seems to be committed to the relationship."

In 1996 Sainsbury's became one of the first retailers to sell Fairtrade products, and now claim to be the world's biggest retailer of such produce. Yet it doesn't seem to promote fair trade towards everyone as they have recently been accused of bully boy tactics by Citigrove Securities and South Ruislip Residents' Association for declaring that they will apply for a judicial review into the planning permission that was legally granted, and signed off by the Mayor of London and our old friend Eric Pickles, the Secretary of State for Communities and Local Government, for a large development in West London on the site of a former dairy that had been a derelict eyesore for ten years. The development includes a cinema, five restaurants and 132 much needed flats and houses. Oh, and an ASDA store. Andrew Rennie of Citigrove Securities was quoted as remarking that "Sainsbury's have had permission to extend their store in South Ruislip since 2006, but have chosen not to do so", and thus believes that the legal challenge "has no merit, but its sole purpose is to stifle and restrict competition".

Unless you've been holidaying on Mars with Colin Pillinger's Beagle 2 probe, no-one could have failed to notice that the big supermarkets are going through a torrid time, and are looking at crisis cutbacks, especially of bigger stores. This though is a crisis of their own making as they didn't respond to the economic downturn and haughtily kept prices high when customers clamoured for alternatives that didn't exist at the time. Experts say that the problem Tesco, in particular, had is that lots of people may well shop there but very few actively love to shop there. Their strategy was a real example of the 'build it and they will come' philosophy, but as the great Motown team Holland, Dozier & Holland wrote (what a creative midfield they would be!) "you can't hurry love... it's a game of give and take". What is galling many, including Rovers fans, is the lack of clarity and openness as to what their intentions for Horfield now are. Sainsbury's favourite tactic seems to be legal delay and obfuscation.

What is worrying is that some Gasheads seem to have already given up the fight. Of course we cannot influence the legal process, which will grind away in the background and hopefully NOT impact on the football side of our performance like it did last season, but there is no reason to suggest that Sainsbury's have a get out of jail free card just because they have an enormous turnover and are a FTSE 100 company. A contract is a contract, and when they entered into it they were extremely happy to secure such a prime piece of real estate. Since then Rovers have bent over backwards to accommodate what are increasingly looking like disingenuous delays to the sale. Little did we know that their range of 'Be Good to Yourself' foods was also the slogan for their own self centred strategy to abrogate responsibilities. If the contract was full of obvious escape clauses they would surely have been long gone by now, like the expensive ring in the Avon.

Gasheads, there is no need to give up the fight yet. Yes, this is more delay. Yes, the Board will not be able to give us a blow by blow account of every legal issue that is going on. But Sainsbury's won't be able to win this just because they can afford a posh lawyer. A well aimed sling shot to the forehead can bring down even the mightiest Philistine Goliath, and if the spoils of war are only a partial fulfillment of the contract, at least we died on our feet rather than lived on our knees.

Viva Zapata, Viva Higgsy. Hasta la victoria siempre!

ACTIVITY TIME

MAKE YOUR OWN SOUNDTRACK TO THE BOOK

- Lead Belly - Goodnight Irene [Every Week]

- any song by Robert Johnson [Week 4]

- The Clash - Should I Stay or Should I Go? [Week 5]

- Sham 69 - If the Kids Are United [Week 11]

- Siouxsie & The Banshees - Dear Prudence [Week 14 - the article doesn't mention The Beatles - I was actually humming the Siouxsie version as I wrote!]

- Ice-T, featuring Jello Biafra - Shut up, be Happy [Week 14]

- Clifford. T. Ward - Home Thoughts From Abroad [Week 39]

- The Supremes - You Can't Hurry Love [Week 39]

- Dinah Washington - What a Diff'rence a Day Makes [Week 42]

- The Velvet Underground - I'm Sticking With You [Week 45]

- The Animals - We've Gotta Get Out of This Place [Week 52]

- The Beatles - Help! [Week 52]

WEEK 40 - THE DARTFORD DOSSIER

PUBLISHED ON WEDNESDAY 4TH FEBRUARY 2015

Saturday 31st January - Conference

Dartford 2   **Bristol Rovers 2**

Hayes - 32', 79'   Taylor - 28', Harrison - 77'

Rovers: Mildenhall, Leadbitter (Dawson - 76'), McChrystal (Capt.) [Booked], Parkes, Brown, Lockyer, Mansell [Booked], Monkhouse, Taylor, Easter (Balanta - 8'), Blissett (Harrison - 60').

Unused Substitutes: Puddy, Trotman, Dawson.

Attendance: 1,832 inc 767 Gas.   Referee: John Brooks

Played 32 Points 58 Position 2nd   *Gap to leaders [Barnet] = 7 points*

The Dartford Dossier

Assistant Manager Marcus Stewart was sent to face the press for the traditional Thursday briefing and said that "we've had them [Dartford] watched and we know what they are all about... No game is the same and you have to approach them all in different ways but the players we have here are brilliant and they all understand what is needed to get the points".

Well clearly the players did NOT know what was needed to get the points, or they ignored the advice they were given and somehow Darrell Clarke and his helpers couldn't drill it into them on the training pitch, before the match, or again at half-time.

I guess the dossier on Dartford, by persons unknown, went something like this... 'This will be part-time Dartford's eighth match in January; twice as many as our full-timers. They have lost nine of their last 10 league games (five by more than a goal) and seem to have only one likelihood of scoring if Harry Crawford fluffs a chance, Tom Bradbrook isn't playing, and his brother Elliott gets stuck in the ground sharing sludge. That one prospect is Ryan Hayes who is very dangerous from set pieces and has already scored direct from his curling corners twice this month. He has a strike rate of almost one in every four games, despite playing on the wing. I would suggest (a) not giving away corners if possible, (b) not giving away close range direct free kicks, and (c) not tinkering around with our goalkeeper, who has done nothing wrong.'

I have consistently supported Darrell Clarke but I am furious that we (apparently) did our homework and then ignored it. Rovers have always been considered a rather light touch and we certainly showed it on Saturday. People may not like what I am about to write but a truly successful team would have forced Hayes off the pitch (rather like Easter was) or at least reduced his effectiveness by not giving him dead ball opportunities. I'm not condoning the former but a ruthless team would have done that if they had to. And a less irresolute goalie wouldn't have looked to the ref for a foul, but would have claimed his territory in the first place and ushered the Dart's player out of the way if necessary. Before anyone shouts 'penalty' at my suggestion of a more aggressive approach, how many penalties have ever been given for a goalie assertively staking his claim in his own six yard box at a corner? I genuinely can't think of one.

If you think I am being overly critical then I guess you have lower standards than myself. I really don't want to see my team in non-league and I will admit I am desperate to get automatic promotion this season. I really don't trust the play-offs, nor a second, third or fourth season in this quagmire. Successful teams strengthen whilst they are near the top, and we haven't done that. Four loan players have left, Ryan Brunt has gone for good, and The Beard, Ollie Clarke and Jermaine Easter are injured, whereas we've only had Mr Easter and two loanees come in.

Darrell was clearly very frustrated in the post-match interview and I applaud him for not blaming the pitch (see photo on page 85). But the buck stops with him. He said "you can't coach individual mistakes" but it was him who consciously decided to put that player back on the pitch.

It is a shame the interviewer wasn't brave enough to ask why a goalkeeper with three clean sheets in four games was 'dropped' for no reason whatsoever except to let a 'big name - big wage' keeper back in. What sort of message does that send out to our squad? That if you are on bigger wages and have played in the Championship you get your place back? That is partly the sort of big headed attitude that got us relegated. It really is. Will Puddy has proved himself just as good as Mildenhall and to discard him sets a bad precedent. He has only let in 5 goals in 8 games this season, and three of those were away to Barnet and Eastleigh (when down to 10 men). He played 42 times in the Conference Premier last season for an average Salisbury City team, kept 11 clean sheets and was named their player's Player of the Season. Just in case the Rovers backroom staff have forgotten, that is the same league that we are now in, so he's hardly the personification of an inexperienced understudy.

I can appreciate that Darrell may have expressed some unwise thoughts when still angry at 5pm, but I loathe to hear him saying "we deserved to win the game" and that "we are the better team". Football is a simple game. No club 'deserves' to win a game when it doesn't score more goals than the opposition. Several Darts fans said that it was their best performance of the season. If so then we just have to deal with that. We need to be 20% better than the opposition if they truly to do "raise their game against Bristol Rovers".

Again I will give credit to our manager for understanding that we have dropped far too many points away from home when ahead, although it has to be said that not only did he forget the fourth example of the phenomenon (1-0 up at Forest Green Rovers, but drew 1-1) but also didn't articulate that he took ultimate responsibility for it. We have dropped eight points away from home from leading positions, but we are being slightly harsh on ourselves on that point as Barnet have dropped nine such points. However, what sets us apart in our respective away performances is not only their 30 points to our 24 (from one game more), but also the fact they've not needed to convert draws into wins often, as they are usually in front anyway! They have a whopping away game goal difference of +12 (it was +17 until two heavy defeats), whereas ours is a faint +1.

Jimmy Hill proposed the three points for a win system and it was introduced in England in 1981. It didn't really catch on elsewhere, and certainly none of the 'big' leagues used it until after it was adopted for the 1994 World Cup Finals. We have had 34 years to get used to it. Away draws may be fine in League Two where three teams get automatic promotion, but too many draws in the Conference can really curtail your chances of that sole, illusive automatic promotion slot.

WEEK 41 - REVERE THE BEARD

PUBLISHED ON TUESDAY 10TH FEBRUARY 2015

Saturday 7th February - Conference

Bristol Rovers 2   Lincoln City 0

Brown - 36', Blissett - 40'

Rovers: Mildenhall, Leadbitter, McChrystal (Capt.), Parkes, Brown, Dawson (Gosling - 89'), Lockyer, Mansell, Monkhouse, Taylor (Balanta - 89'), Blissett (Harrison - 87').

Unused Substitutes: Puddy, Wakefield.

Attendance: 6,528 inc 248 Imps.   Referee: Lee Swabey (3rd time this season)

Played 33 Points 61 Position 2nd   *Gap to leaders [Barnet] = 7 points*

Revere The Beard

A beard is now so fashionable amongst the general populace that it is almost instantly passé.

On the Gaschat forum (no, it's not a pick-up joint for ladies who have a crush on boiler fitters) a legendary thread entitled 'How Tall is the Beard?' currently runs to over 500 replies.

The original post was a photo of a fan with 'The Beard' (midfielder Stuart Sinclair) in Cabot Circus, wondering if the fan was quite tall or 'The Beard' was very small.   The initial replies were vaguely serious but then, following the best tradition of football conversations that meander around and don't have much in common with the original post, they morphed into fabricated one liners showing just how outlandishly amazing 'The Beard' is.   My favourites so far include 'The Prime Minister makes hoax phone calls to Stuart Sinclair', 'He gets so much fan mail he has his own post code', 'The AA call him if they breakdown', 'The speaking clock calls him to find out the time', and obviously 'God prays to Stuart Sinclair'.   If you find none of these amusing, you may need to move on to another blog. They are like buses these days.

Is this reverence just because he has a fisherman's beard? Well, he certainly became an instant cult hero due to his unusual appearance and his amazing enthusiasm for football and BRFC, but he has since also earnt his status through performances. Statistically we have gained more points (1.88 per game) when he has been playing. Until Saturday we only gained 1.50 points per game without him. Of course it is not really possible to compare games solely for one man, but most Gasheads would agree anyway that his energy, tackling, crisp passing and salmon like leap are enough to make him one of the first on the team sheet any day.

Personally I would have had to have a shave, or more likely a shear, if I was trying to play sport professionally, but then again Mr. Sinclair is a very special individual, with very singular powers.

Although people remember the late 1970s and early 1980s as an era of supreme hirsuteness, the reality is that there were still very few players with actual beards. Although many had huge barnets, Forest of Dean style mullets, moustaches that would be more at home in spaghetti western films, and sideboards that resembled off-cuts of carpets, the cheeks and chin were still reserved for 'er indoors to kiss.

The only regular Rovers player I can think of with a proper beard was Stuart Taylor towards the end of his career; a potent symbol of his alpha maleness perhaps? Taylor of course was the 6' 5" Nephilim centre back who holds the record number of League appearances for Rovers (546), a record that given the nature of modern football is very unlikely to be beaten.

Lots of players had moustaches but I'm still struggling find many proper beards on the Eastville grass, the Twerton turf or the Mem's match surface. Top lippers included Mike Green (the captain of the 1973/74 promotion winning team; not the recent goalie with just 2 appearances), Aiden McCaffrey, Paul Randall (particularly in his curly perm phase), Don Gillies, Brian Williams, Paul Bannon, Errington Kelly, Gary Penrice, Kenny Hibbitt, Nigel Martyn and Phil Purnell.

But it wasn't until Bobby Gould's double signing of Ian 'Jocky' Alexander and Geoff Twentyman within one day of each other in late August 1986 that we had possibly the best defensive tasch duo in the whole of the land, with both resembling bushy black slugs or Groucho Marx's thick boot polish imitation. Both went on to make over 300 appearances for the Gas, and Twentyman

Twentyman was remarkably ever-present in the League from Boxing Day 1987 to 23rd August 1991, a staggering 163 games. And if it hadn't been for missing just one game (away to Tranmere Rovers on 23rd August 1991) there would have been 25 more added to that sequence.

There have only been a few attempts I can think of at the Mem, such as Giuliano Grazioli's stubbly look and John French's goatee. Gary Penrice's return in 1997 brought his fluffy top lip back, as if he hadn't realised it was way out of fashion by now. A few years later it was finally, and thankfully, snipped.

Recently Matt Harold and Matt Gill grew quite considerable facial hair for 'Movember'. The former looked like a bit of a tramp, whereas the latter resembled a RAF Brylcreem boy.

As playing with a beard must be hard work it is our off the pitch personalities who have given us some of the most marvellous moments of hirsuteness, courtesy of Barry Bradshaw's massive tasch and black mop of hair, Terry Cooper's luxuriant man hairs and Dennis Booth's walrus like statement of his virility (Dennis was Assistant Manager under John Ward when Ward was still fresh).

But none of them ever matched 'The Beard'.

We need to win every home game we have left, and there is little to fear from the opposition we have left. Our promotion prospects should rest on our away form really, and obviously that of Barnet's.

I don't think it's bigheaded to suggest that Saturday's game was a home banker if ever there was one. Lincoln City came with the unenviable record of merely six points from their last 14 league away games, including three heavy defeats since New Year. Meanwhile Rovers had had a rocket up their bottom last week, and the lush green, green grass of home certainly made a big difference to our play.

After having hit the woodwork four times, and thoroughly dominated the game, a 2-0 win was ultimately narrower than hoped for, but it must have done wonders for the confidence of the 11 on the pitch. It was interesting to see four attacking options and no defenders on the bench; such was the conviction Darrell must have had to force a win by hook or by crook, and his confidence in the flexibility of the players who started should a defensive injury occur.

Amongst the pleasure of watching 16 shots and a comfortable win, it was actually one trifling moment that gave me most delight. I had the perfect sight line for Lee Brown's free kick cracker, and I could see that the Imps had loaded the left hand side of their wall. I was guessing that they had watched Lee Mansell's beautiful right footer from a similar position versus Gateshead, so I prayed that Manse would let Browner take a left footer to exploit the space given. And so it was. How pleasing it is to not only have two excellent free kick takers almost ever present on the pitch (only three league games missed between them), but also for them to be able to leave egos behind and work together for the good of the club.

OI STATS - GOLDFISH BOWL

💀 Who said we couldn't beat the so-called minnows of the division? Although at times it may have seemed that way, we beat all of the bottom eight teams at home, and didn't lose at the Mem to anyone who finished outside the play-offs. The failure to truly dominate away was probably where we lost the title, with a record of W 6 / D 4 / L 2 against teams who finished in the bottom half of the table, and only 2 away wins against teams in the top half.

💀 Rovers scored against every other Conference team in the season.

WEEK 42 - WHAT A DIFF'RENCE A DAY MAKES!

PUBLISHED ON WEDNESDAY 18TH FEBRUARY 2015

Saturday 14th February - Conference

Grimsby Town 0   **Bristol Rovers 1**

Lockyer - 67'

Rovers: Mildenhall, Leadbitter, McChrystal (Capt.), Parkes, Brown, Dawson, Lockyer [Booked], Mansell, Monkhouse, Taylor, Blissett.

Unused Substitutes: Trotman, Wakefield, Gosling, Balanta, Harrison.

Attendance: 4,073 inc 326 Gas.   Referee: Darren England (2nd time this season)

Played 34 Points 64 Position 2nd   *Gap to leaders [Barnet] = 4 points*

What a diff'rence a day makes!

When Dinah Washington collected one of the first ever Grammy awards in 1959, for her performance of a song with an opening gambit of "What a diff'rence a day makes, 24 little hours", it was a shame she couldn't have thanked Wrexham for helping give us that feeling over 55 years later. Washington (whose real name was Ruth Lee Jones; almost the name of an ex-Gas keeper) was known as the 'Queen of the Blues' and the slow melancholy of many of her songs, alongside tracks like Lead Belly's 'Goodnight, Irene', encapsulate how it feels to be a Rovers fan at times. One-part elation, two-parts desolation.

A relatively comfortable win at potentially one of our toughest away fixtures, couple with Barnet losing and the Silkmen only drawing, has put us back into second and suddenly facing a very manageable four point gap to the long-time leaders. Those 24 little hours really have been an injection of optimism in Gasland.

I think we need to win every home game we have left, and then our promotion prospects will rest on our away form, and obviously that of Barnet's and maybe Macclesfield's. Barnet's overall away record may still look very impressive but the Bees are currently in a massive away slump, with three defeats on the trot and only seven points from their last seven trips on the road.

There is a school of thought that says we could actually do better at the higher teams in the league as they may be more likely to want to win the game themselves, and play a more expansive game. It is also possible that some of them have better pitches, which seems to suit our style. Judging from the two impressive wins after the disappointing draw on Dartford's dishevelled dirt track, the pitch issue could well be true. It has to be said though that as Grimsby was our first away win (in six attempts) to a team currently in the Top 10, we are hardly 'ripping up trees' to coin a football expression.

One tiny bonus from the weekend is that John Akinde's sending off for Barnet means he will miss their own crucial game against the Cod Army this Saturday. There must also be a decent chance he could fall foul of the rule which allocates a two match ban for any player who collects 10 yellows before the end of the second Sunday in April (the 11th this season). He is currently on seven, and as he will probably have nine potential games before the cut-off point, the big man may need to tread carefully. Let's hope it effects his game.

I'm all for positivity but some Rovers fans seem to be getting a little ahead of themselves by imagining us top in just over a weeks time, after Barnet have drawn against the Mariners and we have won our two home games within four days. Our games against Altrincham and Braintree Town are perfect banana skins though. If you simply look at their names, and the table, most people will murmur 'home banker', but both are actually in a rich vein of form that belies their 15th and 16th places, respectively. Braintree also have several games in hand on other clubs. Altrincham have 13 points from their last six games, whereas both us and Braintree have 12, so there really is not a lot of choose between us. We are joint top of the home form table, but The Robins and The Iron hold respectable positions in the away form table, at joint sixth, and ninth.

I suspect the pushover performance we gave to Lincoln City may be swapped for the grinding one-goal victories we witnessed earlier in the season (think AFC Telford United, Wrexham, and Dartford) when remarkably Darrell Clarke was fighting for his job. Us Gasheads may be required to demonstrate some patience and not get on anyone's backs if we don't speedily romp into unassailable leads.

Being a Braintree Town fan is an exciting life though. They have only drawn three times this season, none of them away from Cressing Road, and now face a hideous triumvirate of away games at FC Halifax Town, us and Grimsby Town, in a stretch of merely eight days. Let's hope that for once the mainly discredited idea that part-timers suffer when faced with several games (or long away trips) in a short space of time, will finally come true.

By a quirk of fate they are the only two teams left who could potentially do a home and away double over us, as we lost to both away in the first 30 days of the season. Rather surprisingly two teams have already done a double over Barnet, namely Lincoln City and Wrexham. And it would be another great 24 little hours if Grimsby Town dealt them their third next Saturday. Although Grimsby fans are now extremely worried about their promotion chances, and especially their creative abilities, they still have the second meanest defence in the League (after us) and the best away record.

Come on you fish ticklers!

QI STATS - SHIRT NUMBERS

With Gasheads given number 12, and many clubs avoiding number 13, a blue and white number 14 was the shirt number of choice this season with no fewer than four players using it. First it was Jamie White, then Bradley Goldberg, then Josh Wakefield, and finally Chris Lines. I think it would be fair to say that only the last user will be remembered by Gasheads.

Luton Town loanee Dave Martin had number 16 in 2014 before it was used by Jermaine Easter in 2015. Cambridge United loanee Adam Cunnington used 27 until our visit to the Impact Arena (Alfreton Town) and it was handed (still warm) to new signing Nathan Blissett two games later.

Young 'un Donovan Wilson sat on the bench three times in number 28 but it was later taken by Leicester City loanee Adam Dawson, and finally Fulham loanee Lyle-Della Verde was seen sporting number 30 before Abdulai Baggie kept it very clean by never getting to use it on the pitch.

WEEK 43 - BE KIND TO PEOPLE ON THE WAY UP...

EDITED VERSION PUBLISHED ON TUESDAY 24TH FEBRUARY 2015

Saturday 21st February - Conference

Bristol Rovers 1   **Altrincham 0**

Parkes - 45'

Rovers: Mildenhall, Leadbitter, McChrystal (Capt.), Parkes, Brown, Dawson (Gosling - 65'), Lockyer, Mansell [Booked], Monkhouse, Taylor (Harrison - 45'), Blissitt (Balanta - 79').

Unused Substitutes: Puddy, Wakefield.

Attendance: 6,765 inc 162 Robins.   Referee: Brett Huxtable (4th time this season!)

Played 35 Points 67 Position 2nd   *Gap to leaders [Barnet] = 1 point*

Be kind to people on the way up...

As Grimsby Town were becoming the third team in recent weeks to complete a once unlikely league double over Barnet, we were fairly efficiently making sure Altrincham couldn't do the same to us, and are now preparing to face the final team who could potentially inflict such shame upon us, Braintree Town. Should we avoid defeat it will be the first season without a double loss against our name for precisely 20 years, when John Ward's team ended an otherwise excellent season with an agonising Third Tier Play-Off Final defeat at Wembley.

Ward's 1994/95 team let in a misery 40 league goals, only lost once at home, and kept 20 clean sheets. So far in the Conference we have have conceded only 26 goals, only lost once at home, and have kept 17 clean sheets from 35 matches, including nine in the last 13 games.

I love our defence. Parkes and Macca had storming performances against Alty, whilst Lee Brown and Daniel Leadbitter offer a good mixture of defence and attack. Neither is yet good enough to set the world alight, but both are capable players at this level, and could look even better if we 'released' them forward a bit more. I have championed Leadbitter and against Alty he was great, despite some customary panics. Just like Michael Smith a few years ago, his defending is starting to improve, and although he's still young and inexperienced he will be one heck of a player when he learns more about positioning and composure on the ball.

Conceding an average of only 0.74 goals per league game is however not entirely unexpected given the retention of four of the back five that was ranked as the tenth best in League Two last season, plus using a brace of defensive minded central midfielders in front of them. This sadly puts a lot of pressure on the four wider players to be creative though, and the front two to score goals, as neither Sinclair, Mansell, Clarke nor Lockyer are likely to score many from open play (8 such goals in 86 midfield appearances). If we can get the balance right I think we could still win this league.

I was really surprised when I bobbed onto the Barnet fans forum over the last few weeks to read some considerable dislike aimed towards us, and various extremely arrogant attitudes about how they are going to walk the league. They were even naming the game when they would receive the Conference title! This was not just Internet bravado either; these were serious feelings that they had pretty much already won the league and that heroes like John Akinde and Martin Allen would display typical testosterone fuelled brawn to bulldoze their way through any opposition, just as they did in the first half of the season.

This macho invincibility has been slowly unravelling since New Year though, with Akinde not only scoring less goals, but less important goals, and also getting sent off for a dive and missing their crucial defeat against Grimsby Town on Saturday. And Allen is now being criticised as a one tactic pony, who is refusing to see the problems that the more cerebral and mature posters on their forum are clearly pointing out. To be fair Allen is actually a two trick pony, as he seems to have one line-up (with more flair) for the Hive, and another for away matches. Other than that weekly adjustment he just seems to be ploughing the same furrow, over and over again.

One Bees fan reasoned that they will win the league because Martin Allen had experience of being top virtually all season with Gillingham in 2012/13 and safely getting them over the League Two finishing line, whereas neither Darrell Clarke or Paul Hurst (Grimsby Town) had. Well, without trying to diminish the fact that Allen deserves immense credit for that promotion, this jolly Bee forgot to note that the Gills actually won only four of their final 13 games, and they were all narrow home wins; which is hardly inspiring as we come into the last dozen games of THIS season. And of course anyone who could be bothered to summon up the energy to type 'Darrell Clarke' or 'Paul Hurst' into a browser will instantaneously spot two hard fought promotions on both of their CV's. Arrogant? Surely not.

Wilson Mizner led a frankly outlandish life, and during it came up with many now celebrated bon mots, including "Be kind to people on the way up; you'll meet the same people on the way down", which rather reminds me of Barnet. A few dozen fans on a forum will not always represent a club's wider fan base of course, so I am willing to give them the benefit of the doubt, but these negative comments about us sound even more peculiar as there is no 'history' between us, or animosity.

In fact the final Football League encounter between us, in front of over 8,500 on a Friday night under the lights at the Mem in February 2013, may have seen Ryan Brunt snatch an extra time winner that leap-frogged us out of the relegation zone and over Barnet, but many Rovers fans actually went home acclaiming Edgar David's Barnet as the best and most positive team we'd seen in Horfield that season. You could certainly see how they held the rather curious honour of beating the top and second teams in the division on their own turf. At the end of that season Gasheads were saddened to see the Bees relegated, and in a situation rather like us a year later, it was only on goal difference and with a whopping 51 points. That tally would have kept them up in every other season since automatic relegation began in 1986/87.

We've only ever met them 16 times, and the only real history is of us letting Giuliano Grazioli go to them in June 2003 as part of a player plus £110,000 swap for Manuel 'Junior' Agogo. Sadly for us it was other clubs who poached even more gifted players from them, such as Albert Adomah and Jason Puncheon. Barnet, like many smaller London clubs, tend to benefit from their location when picking up talented youngsters discarded by the Premier League perennials, or even players who just like the trappings of the big City that they call home.

It has been suggested that opposition teams raise their game against any league leaders, have 'worked Barnet out', and will work us out if we reach those heady heights. That may be true to some degree, but it would be a sorely shallow and shoddy analysis of a much more complex wobble, and just like Mr. Allen, anyone whose research stops at that sound bite would seem to be absent mindedly admiring a beautiful African sunset whilst sailing on a felucca down the longest river in the world (i.e. in denial). Barnet's problems seem to be deeper than that, as a worryingly leaky defence is being married with a distinct lack of pace on the wings. Forum bees seem to be calling for the youthful exuberance of Mauro Vilhete and Luke Gambin on the wings, and the undoubtedly talented, but ponderous, Luisma Villa Lopez moving into the middle. Meanwhile last season's top scorer, the mercurial Keanu Marsh-Brown, has been cold shouldered by Allen and took to twitter before Saturday's match to comment, "What a waste of a season". Classy.

As for us becoming 'the hunted' if we ever get to be leaders, well, as the newly relegated club with the largest fan base in the league we have possibly been that every game this season anyway, so hopefully that will not be a reason for us to fail if we get there.

What I find strange is why no-one is talking about Macclesfield Town. To see this as a two horse race is bordering on the disdainful. There is no evidence to suggest that the Silkmen could not potentially win this league. I get a feeling no-one is mentioning them solely because they are not, (a) a team who have been top of the league nearly all season, and have a 26 goal top scorer, or (b) a team with large attendances, some decent players, a good young manager, and a passion to right the wrongs we committed last season. If their chances are to be judged solely on watching them once this season, taking a tonking from us 4-0 (incidentally their last loss), then of course many of us will scratch our heads and wonder how on earth they can be up there, but judged purely on statistics, especially when holding the joint best home record in the league and being top of the current form table, the Silkmen should be kept under vigilant surveillance.

Next, Braintree Town, and I won't complain at another 1-0 grind if necessary.

WEEK 44 - BEWARE THE IDES OF MARCH

PUBLISHED ON WEDNESDAY 3RD MARCH 2015

Tuesday 24th February - Conference

Bristol Rovers 2   **Braintree Town 1**

Taylor (pen) - 31', Harrison - 83'   Akinola - 38'

Rovers: Mildenhall, Leadbitter, Brown, McChrystal (Capt.), Parkes, Lockyer (Dawson - 72' [Booked]), Mansell [Booked], Gosling (Balanta - 46'), Monkhouse [Booked], Taylor, Blissett (Harrison - 61').

Unused Substitutes: Puddy, Wakefield.

Attendance: 6,471 inc 23 Brainers.   Referee: Dean Treleaven (2nd time this season)

Saturday 28th February - Conference

Gateshead 0   **Bristol Rovers 1**

Harrison - 71'

Rovers: Mildenhall, Leadbitter, McChrystal (Capt.), Parkes, Brown, Lockyer, Mansell, Monkhouse, Sinclair (Dawson - 28'), Taylor (Harrison - 64'), Blissett.

Unused Substitutes: Puddy, Trotman, Balanta.

Attendance: 1,668 inc 667 Gas.   Referee: Ian Hussin

Played 37 Points 73 Position 1st   *Gap to 2nd place [Barnet] = 2 points, but they had a game in hand*

Beware the Ides of March

Well, we did it.

We reached the top. For the first time since 11th March 2000.

Of course we are under no illusions that we will stay there all the way until late April, but we certainly stand a better chance than our infamous implosion under Ian Holloway 15 years ago and I'd certainly prefer to have our league stats (20 matches unbeaten, 15 matches unbeaten away from home, one loss in 30 matches, best home record in the division), than the inconsistency of most of the other clubs around us.

The team that, until a weekend thrashing, could not be considered to be inconsistent was Macclesfield Town, partly because they were unbeaten in the six games since we flayed them alive at Christmas, but partly because last week they couldn't play either of their games, so despite us only squeaking successive home victories at least we got them 'in the bag'. Add to that another crucial 1-0 win at Gateshead (our eighth 1-0 of the season) and our stats now almost match those of Gerry Francis's all conquering 1990 Third Tier Champions; we are just two points and six goals short after 37 games, whilst both had a miserly defence that had conceded only 27 goals.

Gateshead and FC Halifax Town are also still a tad of an unknown quantity as they have so many games in hand, and Halifax not only have most of the top teams left to play (including us once and Barnet twice), but have only played five league games since 2014 and their pitch currently resembles the practise ground of the West Yorkshire Young Yokels Ploughing Club.

Whilst the Shaymen's pasture may be causing furrowed brows, the Mem could almost host the Crown Green Bowls World Cup, and is surely helping us to play our own game in these crucial home matches against so-called 'easy' opposition.

It is probably helping the opposition as well though, as the stereotype of the lumpen non-league player seems to be sorely out-of-date, especially for midfielders and wide players. With Alan Devonshire in charge it was hardly unexpected that Braintree Town would possess some skilful players. Devonshire was one of my boyhood heroes of a West Ham United team oozing a mix of East end iron (Lampard Snr, Billy Bonds, Ray Stewart, Alvin Martin, etc) and skill and guile (Trevor Brooking, Paul Allen and Dev). But like so many in football, his break almost never came, being discarded twice by Crystal Palace as a youngster (the second time by future Rovers manager Malcolm Allison) and ending up playing for Southall in his spare time and fork lift driving at the amazing art-deco Hoover building on the A40 by day. West Ham did finally spot him, aged 20, and that was that for 14 years of a celebrated career.

Obviously Simeon Akinola could not fail to catch the eye with his devastating pace and athleticism, and I cannot remember the last time an opposition player was applauded for his goal rather than chided for celebrating near the raucous North Terrace. Watford's Bernard Mensah also looked a handful, back again on loan with the Iron after only being used sparingly by Barnet when on loan there earlier in the season.

Until 44 BC, the Ides (15th) of March was pretty much as standard for the Roman Republic of the era; a day of religious sacrifice, plus the incomparable Feast of Anna Perenna, where the plebs got to have a yearly booze up that seems to have resembled our snogging of strangers on New Year's Eve. When a seer warned Julius Caesar that harm would come to him by the time of the Ides of March, the big man may well have scoffed, but on that fateful day he was indeed assassinated, by his own senators.

March could well be a tough month for us, although I somehow doubt Darrell Clarke will be uttering 'Et tu, Higgsy?'. We host potentially our hardest home opponents remaining (Eastleigh), and although Aldershot Town may not look like a testing game on paper, games against relegation threatened clubs are always hard at this stage of the season, and frankly every promotion contender has a smattering of them. Add to this mix probably our two most arduous away games, as we visit Macclesfield Town, who have the second best home record this season (after us), and FC Halifax Town, who have the third best, although their credentials are somewhat incomplete as they still have four of the top six to play.

Looking back to last season's Conference battle, leaders Luton Town had an unusually poor March 2014, with three wins, two draws and a brace of defeats. That may not sound too bad until you realise that those were their first defeats since early September, that they had won all four matches in February (2-1, 7-0, 5-0 and 5-0 again!), and overall had won 12 out of the previous 13 games, with a goal difference of +40. Some of those figures may resonate this season with statistically minded Gasheads! Despite this sticky patch their lead only reduced by a solitary point as several teams stumbled, including Barnet, who earned only four points from six matches during March and dropped from third place to ninth.

Personally I think we have nothing to get edgy about. We have got far higher that anyone expected this season and I still think the pressure is on Barnet, especially until they use their game in hand, as many of their fans are still bullish that they hold their own destiny in their hands. We certainly are struggling to win easily, but we are winning, and a thousand football teams all over the globe would love to be in that situation.

WEEK 45 - HOW DID THEY RE-FLOAT A MAROONED PIRATE BOAT?

EDITED VERSION PUBLISHED ON TUESDAY 10TH MARCH 2015

Saturday 7th March - Conference

Bristol Rovers 1
Taylor - 79'

Eastleigh 2
Green - 7', Midson - 63'

Rovers: Mildenhall, Leadbitter (Blissett - 45' [Booked]), McChrystal (Capt.), Parkes, Brown, Dawson (Balanta - 65'), Lockyer, Mansell (Clarke - 87'), Monkhouse, Taylor, Harrison.

Unused Substitutes: Puddy, Trotman.

Attendance: 7,371 inc 233 Spitfires.   Referee: Steven Rushton (3rd time this season)

Played 38 Points 73 Position 1st   *Gap to 2nd place [Barnet] = 2 points, but they had a game in hand*

Note - the following article deliberately arose from of a consultation exercise I did on the two main Rovers Internet fan forums. I gave fans seven possible 'turning points' / important factors of our season so far, and asked people to vote for the ones they thought were most important. I also asked for any comments / suggestions.

The following is my full version of the article. I also produced a heavily edited version for my weekly blog on the Bristol Post web site.

How did they re-float a marooned pirate boat?

Last week I asked Gasheads on the two main Rovers Internet forums to vote which of the following seven factors have been most important in our turnaround this season. Some are clear events or turning points, whilst other are more timeless factors. After over 250 votes, here are the results from the Pirateland jury.

I also asked for comments and extra suggestions. The most recurring offering was the televised 3-2 come back win against Gateshead just before Christmas, so I've added this at the close as a 'wild card'. To be clear, I wasn't arrogantly suggesting we have won the league. I was just trying to look back over 40 hard games and see when things started going right for us (for once), and why.

1) Sticking like glue (31% of votes) - After the Braintree Town loss in early September we were 15th in the table, with eight points from seven matches, and there was a strong rumour that Darrell Clarke could be gone if the following Tuesday night match against Wrexham didn't go well. We won 1-0, the second of eight 'Arsenal scores' so far this season, and Darrell stayed. The great Velvet Underground drummer Mo Tucker was not much of a singer, but her brace of contributions included a delightfully childish ditty that went "I'm sticking with you, 'cause I'm made out of glue". Very apt.

2) The tale of two centre backs (26%) - A team will rarely concede only 0.73 goals a game, and earn 18 clean sheets out of 37 games, without a good centre back pairing, and although this hasn't been a single decisive moment as such, a negative turning point was potentially averted because we've boasted not just one top class partnership, but two. At this late stage of the season it is easy to forget that Tom Parkes, one of only two ever presents in the league this season and an early candidate for Player of the Season, was actually partnered by Neal Trotman for 16 out of the first 19 games, until Trots was injured at AFC Telford United and replaced by Mark McChrystal. Macca has been Parkes' ever improving partner for all of the 19 league games since, and amazingly they have picked up only seven yellow cards, and no reds, between all three of them.

More precise turning points could be two specific draws that central defenders helped earn for us. A point at Wrexham in early December was disappointing in some respects, but having Macca in goal for 50 minutes (after Mildy was injured) and still keeping a clean sheet should never be sniffed at. We may not have had a sub keeper, but surely in Neal Trotman we had one of the best central defenders ever to have graced a Conference bench, and between them the three central defender musketeers helped earn what may prove to be a crucial point.

Similarly if Rovers get into the play-offs by a point, or even win the league by that little digit, we might wish to send a Methuselah of Champagne to Torquay United's foolish centre back Angus MacDonald. The Gulls (or should that be the Turkeys?) were the best team I've seen at the Mem this until we grabbed a barely deserved late New Years' Day point courtesy of a few moments of madness; two yellows within 11 minutes for MacDonut and a gifted penalty.

3) Take the honey and run - a.k.a. The Spiegel & Mensah Bequest (14%) - At the time it felt like only a pyrrhic victory, as we were still 8 points behind Barnet (albeit with a game in hand) and didn't actually reduce the gap below five points until mid-February, but that last-gasp winner versus Barnet on a wet Tuesday evening in late November 2014 was exactly the physical and psychological win we needed to keep us within a fighting distance of the honeydrippers.

If we do get promotion I think we will have to inaugurate a 'Spiegel & Mensah Bequest', which could be bestowed on the opposing players who have helped us most that season. Swiss Under 21 goalkeeper Raphael Spiegel was rather bizarrely picked up by the Barnet team coach at Reading Services on the way along the M4 to the match. The West Ham United loanee was thrust into this crucial game and should be very disappointed at the way Matty Taylor's opening goal went past him at his near post. There was also a question mark about how the last gasp winner from Angelo Balanta got past the 6' 6" debutant. A Barnet fan recently told me that Agent ~~Keyser Soze~~ Spiegel was never seen again at Barnet. As the poet Charles Baudelaire wrote, 'The finest trick of the Devil is to persuade the world that Raphael Spiegel exists'.

Later in the season Watford's Bernard Mensah looked a handful upfront when paired out wide with Simeon Akinola for Braintree Town. As Mensah is quite a common Ghanaian name I dared not assume that he was the same Mensah that was on loan at Barnet earlier in the season, but after a trip onto the Internet the evidence said it was. A week later, as I revisited the highlights of the Barnet win, I almost felt like he was following me around, as I witnessed him standing completely still as 'his man', Balanta, made a front post run, nay a jog, rose unchallenged and nodded in the goal that may have turned our season. As Mensah had been on the pitch less than 30 minutes I have no idea what tired old excuse he could use for his total inactivity at the crucial corner. As the ball bounced over to him after the goal, he smashed it like a rugby player over the stand in frustration. If only he had shown such vigour a few seconds earlier! Well done Agent Mensah.

4) LDV and Tricky Dawso (10%) - Let's be honest, we've still never achieved a 'proper / balanced' squad of our own players as we've never had a creative midfielder and never had pace on the wings. I won't include 'goal scorers' in this complaint because like it or not, we've always physically had numerous forwards at the club. Whether they have been the right people at the right time is a moot point of course, but that is a separate question to this 'turning point'. I'm also not going to be pernickety enough to complain, for example, that we don't have cover for Lee Brown at left-back, because many teams (especially those in non-league) are not going to have perfect cover for every position, and acquiring utility players who can fill in (as Tom Lockyer did for Brown's three league absences so far) is just as much a skill of management than having that perfect centre forward who scores loads of goals and is never injured or suspended.

ANYWAY, to get to the point, the signing of attacking wingers on loan is offered as this third turning point. The first man in, Dave Martin from Luton Town, didn't quite go to plan despite an impressive start, but Lyle Della-Verde from Fulham was a fan's favourite until injured, and in 2015 Leicester City's Adam Dawson has proved just as tricky and attack minded. These wingers have offered us something different and certainly have become the creative outlet we don't possess in our own squad. Crucially Dawson arrived at time when Daniel Leadbitter is been used as a more attacking right back, so we now have a very creative and pacy right side, coupled with a more steady and prosaic left hand side.

5) No fireworks since Guy Fawkes' Night (8%) - Another minor turning point was at the away game at FC Telford United on 1st November, which saw our fifth, and final, red card of the season so far, as well as the return of Tom Lockyer after a one match ban for five yellow cards. That plethora of cards in the first 19 games could have left casual observers wondering if our players had a serious discipline problem. It didn't seem so, as none of them were for awful challenges, but it was most probably costing us points, as we only garnered four points from the four games where we had players dismissed. Up to that game at the New Bucks Head we were earning 1.77 points per game. Since that game we have plundered 2.21 points per league game and hadn't lost until this weekend. Co-incidence?

6) A Roman salute (7%) - Whilst most people were Christmas shopping in mid December, 3,500 hardy souls were watching our old friends from Bath City deservedly beat us in the First Round of a cup that I frankly thought could be bolstering our sparse trophy cabinet; a possible consolation prize when missing out on promotion. This F.A. Trophy result, and performance, sent some Rovers fans into a melodramatic meltdown, just like Eastleigh has now, but the defeat was not really a big shock, against a team only one division lower and with us fielding a team that was not only weakened and rusty, but just as importantly had not regularly played together. Avoiding a potentially long and winding journey on muddy winter pitches was most probably a godsend. In retrospect the old axiom that the only good time to go out of such a competition is either at the First Round or the Wembley final seems painfully true.

7) Leaving our Brains in the gutter (4%) - If our first eight days in the Conference Premier were traumatic (1 point from 3 games), our final away defeat (so far) was maybe the extra, if belated, lesson in humility we needed. Thankfully the season lasts eight months, not eight days, and seven points from our second trio of matches started to put a nice gloss on our new surroundings. But providence had one more jolt for us. A 2-0 defeat at Braintree Town was our final low point, and a few of our fans put us back in the headlines for all the wrong reasons, whilst the press ignored the dedication of the 500+ others on the longest trip of the season thus far. Thankfully our fans have mainly received good press since, including a lovely thank you note from the Eastleigh chairman, national sympathy at some Gasheads being locked out by Woking, and the staggering statistic that Gasheads have supplied an average of 31% of the total crowd on our away trips.

Wild Card

Knock down? What knock down? - Like a fighter who just doesn't know when he's beat, Rovers proved against Gateshead that not only could they reply to the criticism they faced after losing to Bath City the week before, but were now a team who knew they had the craft and the guts to potentially win any game of football. The motto seemed to be; 'If you take the lead twice, we'll just score three!' Rovers notched up a trio of absolutely wonderful goals (indeed, with all five goals being quality, the head honcho at BT Sport must have been licking his lips) and yet again Darrell Clarke made a brave early change when things weren't panning out the way he had expecting them to. It was like the famous Liverpool - Newcastle match in 1996, when the team from the opposite bank of the Tyne were ahead twice but Liverpool still came back to win 4-3.

WEEK 46 - CAME AS A NEUTRAL, LEFT AS A FAN

PUBLISHED ON WEDNESDAY 18TH MARCH 2015

Saturday 14th March - Conference

FC Halifax Town 2
Maynard - 25', Roberts - 39'

Bristol Rovers 2
Brown - 83', Harrison - 89'

Rovers: Mildenhall, Leadbitter, Lockyer (Easter - 64'), McChrystal (Capt.), Parkes, Brown, Clarke (Harrison - 52'), Mansell, Lines, Monkhouse, Taylor (Balanta - 75').

Unused Substitutes: Puddy, Dawson.

Attendance: 2,248 inc 668 Gas.   Referee: Darren England (3rd time this season)

Played 39 Points 74 Position 2nd   Same points as leaders [Barnet], but they had a better Goal Difference and a game in hand.

Came as a neutral, left as a fan

Away games do funny things to a person. One of my brothers took a friend along to the FC Halifax Town match at the weekend. It was only the second live match Maki had ever been to, and her first taste of Gas.

At 2-0 down and staring at a pitch more akin to a turnip field than a theatre of nocturnal imaginings, it wouldn't be unfair to assume that our honoured guest may have been rather under-whelmed. But football often truly is a game of two halves, and with belated creative and attacking subs finally permitted onto the pitch by a disappointedly distrustful Darrell Clarke, a storming comeback saw the boys in blue steal a point and almost make it all three in the dying seconds. Ellis Harrison's leveller had shades of van Basten about it, and had it been executed on a lush Premier League pitch it would have unquestionably been replayed umpteen times, analysed from every camera angle, and slobbered over by hideously overpaid pundits.

That final ten minutes had my brother's fellow traveller more excited than at any time this year, remarking that she went into the ground as a neutral, but came out as a fan.

You can't really get a higher accolade than that, and the team spirit and heart shown when down and almost out is one of many reasons why despite being in the Conference, Pirates have still flocked to away games this season. The 22 away games so far have witnessed an average of 760 Gasheads per game, and the average distance to each match has been a whopping 294 mile round trip (from Bristol). The reward has been an unbeaten away run of 16 league matches, although points have never come easy, with only a solitary two goal win, and having to come from behind in three matches.

With 16,718 Gashead travellers so far, in an overall attendance of only 54,112 (less than those who are present at a single Arsenal match; that makes you stop and think!), it means that Pirates have made up 31% of the crowd. At Dorchester Town Gasheads comprised 60% of the crowd, and at Forest Green Rovers we were just a handful away from supplying half the crowd, at 49.9% (for an all-ticket, Bank Holiday match as well). Those statistics may even yet be beaten as two mammoth followings are expected at Kidderminster Harriers and Dover Athletic. A full list of away day stats is available on the final page of the book (page 189).

Add into the mix the fact that six of the games were all-ticket, four were on Tuesday evenings (at an average round trip of 258 miles), and two were on Bank Holidays, then it seems even more remarkable that Gasheads travel to away games in such large numbers.

Of course not all away travellers will be travelling from Bristol, and the larger than average Gas away following to matches in the London and South-East area obviously suggests there are quite a few travelling Gasheads who probably live in that part of the UK. However, it would be equally unwise to suppose that Rovers aren't most probably extremely average when plotting where its exiled fans live. From anecdotal evidence gathered when I edited and sold the 'Away The Gas' book, Gasheads are spread out over the whole country, especially in many major conurbations, but we also have a huge raft in local areas, particularly North and East Bristol, Keynsham, and South Gloucestershire. No surprises there really.

So what makes away games so special? The old adage that 'it's better to travel than arrive' (a mutation of Robert Louis Stevenson's "To travel hopefully is a better thing than to arrive...") is so apt for proper away rovers. I still get a sense of adventure going away, especially to a ground I've never been to before. Part of the fun of away grounds is getting lost, wandering into an awful boozer, and seeking out the local ale and grub (oatcakes in the Potteries, oven bottom muffins around Oldham and Stockport, fresh pasties out of the back of a van at Plymouth), although increasingly these days there is no food near a ground due to the industrial park wasteland localities that have infiltrated our proud quest.

When travelling away you know you'll be in the company of hard-core Gasheads and famished exiles, and most will want to sing and have a laugh. You don't go to away games for a guaranteed win so you might as well not treat the game too seriously and find something to distract you from the probable result. I usually end up looking at silly haircuts or funny signs. Enough said.

Away days rule ok, and may their special alchemy continue to turn neutrals into fans for a very long time yet!

OI STATS - GAS ON TOUR

☠ The Rovers support at Aldershot (1,255) was larger than the TOTAL crowd at seven out of the 11 other Conference games that Saturday. I suspect several other weekends were like that as well, but that was the one I wrote down at the time.

☠ Rovers fans officially outnumbered the home fans at Dorchester Town (FA Cup), Welling United, Nuneaton Town, Kidderminster Harriers and Dover Athletic. And made up 49.9% of the crowd at FGR!

☠ Although our away following was generally amazing, we took less supporters to three clubs (Grimsby Town, Lincoln City & Wrexham) than they brought to us.

☠ A full list of away day stats is available on the final page of the book (page 189).

WEEK 47 - THEY DON'T LIKE IT UP 'EM!

PUBLISHED ON THURSDAY 26TH MARCH 2015

Friday 20th March - Conference

Bristol Rovers 3

Easter - 13', Monkhouse - 59',
Taylor - 61'

Aldershot 1

Williams - 32'

Rovers: Puddy, Leadbitter, McChrystal (Capt.) [Booked], Parkes, Brown, Dawson [Booked], Lockyer, Lines (Clarke - 90'), Monkhouse, Taylor (Balanta - 82'), Easter (Harrison - 70').

Unused Substitutes: Mildenhall, Blissett.

Attendance: 7,416 inc 235 Shots. Referee: Ben Toner (2nd time this season)

Played 40 Points 77 Position 2nd *Gap to leaders [Barnet] = 1 point*
(after all weekend matches played)

They Don't Like it Up 'Em!

Before Friday's match Chris Barker, Aldershot's Caretaker Manager and journeyman Centre Back spoke about his stereotypically lazy game plan of slowing Rovers down in the first 20-30 minutes so that "hopefully the crowd will turn on them".

Maybe I'm being too harsh on an inexperienced manager seemingly faced with a lack of tactical options when visiting the team second in the league, and who boast average home crowds more than double the nearest competitor, but it strikes me that many professionals who you expect will do their own research are often actually just trotting out tired clichés that they have presumably heard from others, and have certainly not bothered to test any evidence behind such an erroneous belief.

The best method to swat away this bunkum is simply to keep on winning, and makes me recall Dad's Army's eccentric Lance-Corporal Jones and his catchphrases 'Don't Panic!' and, in reference to his old school love of bayonet warfare, 'They don't like it up 'em!'.

I'm not suggesting that Gasheads are perfect and never get stressed, but to suggest that our fans are harming our chances on the field seems to defy logic when we have the best home record in the league, and a 16 match unbeaten away record, which is easily the longest run in the top five leagues.

Whilst there certainly is nervousness amongst the Rovers faithful, it has mainly been kept in check, often by excellent mid-game tactical changes, late goals, and the use of benches that often seem to have more attacking and creative quality upon them than the starting XI actually possess.

It seems particularly perverse that whilst analytical pundits such as Radio 5's 'Non-League Football Show' are applauding us for our humility this season, many lesser commentators are just perpetuating myths that have been circling for far too long. Whilst we have swiftly learnt the hard lessons Luton Town took five seasons to ascertain, it seems as if it is now our opponents who have failed to keep up with the times.

This season has rarely been an easy ride for Gasheads yet we are second in the league. It has been a pretty miserable experience being a Pirate for the previous four seasons, and also most of the last 15 seasons, so there has undoubtedly been considerable pressure and a lot of tension in the air since that fateful relegation last May.

We may have seen some decent away results and certainly a very impressive unbeaten run but not many games have really been exciting. There haven't been any comfortable, non-stressful league games on the road, except maybe Nuneaton Town (our sole two goal away win). Long and thin open terraces haven't helped and at times it has been hard for even the most positive and numerous fans to create a high-class atmosphere in those situations.

At home it would also have been nice to have had a few more games where people could relax a bit and enjoy it. The only relatively 'easy' victories I can remember were Macclesfield Town (4-0), Lincoln City (2-0) and Nuneaton Town (3-1), and even then we were momentarily rocked by The Boro coming back to 2-1 and putting us under pressure for a while.

Similar happened against the Shots on Friday. Brett Williams is considered to be one of the best strikers in the Conference and although his only chance came via the type of defensive lapse that has become all too prevalent in the last three games, his goal unsettled us after a stunning start and reinstated depression back into the minds of the loyal 7,000+. But heads did not drop and a brace of exciting goals within a few minutes of each other led to the first relaxed, nay dull, final half an hour of football for a long time.

Our two experienced signings, Jermaine Easter and Chris Lines, both really caught the eye. Whilst we now have more creativity and skill going forward than at any other point this season, we paradoxically have seen the defence creaking like never before.

I suspect there will still be twists and turns in the tile race yet, but I am a lot more confident (even for the play-offs) with Easter and Linesy in the team, as performers who could potentially 'unlock' a stubborn defence, especially on a day when not everything is going for us.

Although Stuart Sinclair and Lee Mansell were undoubtedly missed as the midfield steel under the lights, suspensions or injuries are circumstances that most teams will have to deal with at this time of the season. For example, there is a chance we could be dealing with a severely depleted Southport team in three weeks time as their discipline is horrendous, with top scorer Richard Brodie, and central defender pairing Luke Foster and Luke George, currently sharing a staggering 36 yellow cards between them and all facing bans if further misdemeanors are committed. And with Barnet only taking six points in the seven games when John Akinde has been booked (and he himself only scoring twice), there is a prospect that a possible ban could weigh on his mind soon.

WEEK 48 - WHERE THERE IS UNITY THERE IS STRENGTH

PUBLISHED ON WEDNESDAY 1ST APRIL 2015

Saturday 28th March - Conference

Macclesfield Town 0   Bristol Rovers 0

Rovers: Puddy, Leadbitter, McChrystal (Capt.), Parkes, Brown, Balanta (Dawson - 68'), Lockyer, Lines, Monkhouse, Taylor, Easter (Blissett - 79').

Unused Substitutes: Mildenhall, Clarke, Baggie.

Attendance: 2,591 inc 782 Gas.   Referee: Martin Coy

Played 41 Points 78 Position 3rd   *Gap to leaders [Barnet] = 1 point*
(after all weekend matches played)

Where there is unity there is strength

It's that time of the year again and the BRFC 1883 Sponsors Club is upon us.

If you are wondering what on earth that is you won't be looked down upon (much), as it is primarily aimed at businesses rather than terrace dwellers like you and I.   But it does affect us, the supporters, as it determines what sponsor will be emblazoned on the famous blue and white quarters next season, as well at the less famous yellow / white / purple / black / green / orange away kit (delete as applicable).

For £1,200 a pop 'sponsors' get entered into a draw to win one of five prizes, including their name / logo as the sponsor for the whole season on the home kit, the away kit or the back of the shorts.   And to significantly sweeten the odds every sponsor gets a very generous hospitality package, a signed football, and their name up in miniature lights in every programme and on the club web site.

At this point it may seem as if this is an advertorial for the club I support, but bear with me, there are two clear reasons why this deserves column inches, and why my independence can still always be guaranteed.

As an economic slump hit the country in the late 2000's, and Rovers confronted the end of an 11 year marriage of convenience to Cowlin Construction, football sponsorship was exactly the kind of expense a lot of belt-tightening businesses could painlessly chop. Justifying say £50,000 to £100,000 to sponsor a relative minnow was getting harder and harder and several football clubs even ended up with no sponsor on their shirt at all. Like a rogue landlord who didn't want to reduce the rent on their flea pit, they cut their nose off to spite their face, worried that a cut-price deal would forever see prospective sponsors expecting bargain deals, even when the economy had recovered; which would be next year, wouldn't it?

Of course we now know the recovery didn't happen the next year, nor the following years, which re-iterated just how prescient the Rovers idea was, as it still delivers the goods seven seasons later. At the time of conception in 2009 the 1883 Sponsors Club was a very innovative idea and one we can be proud of. It was spectacularly successful, with all 96 slots sold, and was subsequently copied by other sporting clubs.

So, what's to stop an innovative offer being taken up by another innovative club? Well, nothing. Which is why it is quite amazing that within just the last few weeks the 'Fans Forum Sponsor Club' (FFSC) has managed to raise the necessary lolly to enter the draw for next season. The FFSC was started in January 2013 by ordinary, run of the mill fans on the official BRFC Internet forum in order to support the club, primarily through sponsorship of matches and of players who may not normally attract a backer. For just £10 a season a club 'member' would not just get the warm fuzzy feeling of financially supporting the club they follow, but also the chance to win various prizes such as hospitality places at sponsored games, and the actual shirts of the players they had been sponsoring. As the idea snowballed the impact was amazing, especially on young players.

Can you imagine how it must feel to be a younger footballer knowing that all the well-known names in the squad have their kits sponsored by businesses, pubs and the odd individual Gashead, whereas yours most probably won't be? But one day along comes a member of the BRFC back-room staff and tells you that the Fans Forum have chosen to sponsor yours! That must make you feel on top of the world, and really part of a close-knit relationship between young players and fans.

Off the pitch many FFSC members have met new friends, which is entirely fitting considering one of its aims is to encourage unity and positivity. Ex-players Devon White and Christian McClean have been staggered at the interest shown in them when they were invited to be FFSC guests at games.

Unfortunately the football club didn't spend money wisely last season and a catalogue of errors ended in relegation, despite the best efforts of loyal, genuine, and generous Rovers fans all over the world. In the face of that kick in the teeth, and the shocking unilateral closure of the official Internet forum once the Board decided they didn't want to face the criticism of their inept servitude of a 131 year-old club, the FFSC has survived. It has now raised an astonishing £11,500 for the club so far, and this season has sponsored nine players, many of them youngsters and new arrivals.

It's not too late to join the FFSC - details are available on the various Rovers Internet forums.

Meanwhile on the pitch the twists and turns continue with Rovers disappointingly now third, but no further away from Barnet. Whilst the performance at 4th place Macclesfield Town was hardly inspiring, it was probably the hardest game that any of the top four had left to play. Bees and Pirates both seemed to feel their teams played poor, but what both results showed was that no team in this division is dominant away from home, and one goal leads are always suspect. The Bees hold a connected, and unwanted, stat; the first day of November was the last time they won an away game without being two goals ahead at some point in the match. Since then they have squandered winning positions three times, and have only 15 away points from a possible 33 (Grimsby Town have 24, and we have 19).

Despite our 17 match unbeaten away run, draws are still costing us and we only have the 6th best away record in the league. Wins at Kidderminster Harriers and Dover Athletic are now imperative, and another kick in the teeth from that old devil called 'Goal Difference' will not be welcomed after last years' calamity.

WEEK 49 - GOODNIGHT BEN

PUBLISHED ON WEDNESDAY 8TH APRIL 2015

Good Friday 3rd April - Conference

Bristol Rovers 5

Taylor - 15', Heneghan (og) - 26',
Monkhouse - 33', 83', Harrison - 88'

Chester FC 1

McBurnie - 60'

Rovers: Puddy, Leadbitter, Lockyer, Parkes, Brown, Dawson (McChrystal - 75'), Mansell (Capt.), Lines, Monkhouse, Taylor (Blissett - 85'), Easter (Harrison - 27').

Unused Substitutes: Mildenhall, Balanta.

Attendance: 8,455 inc 348 Seals.   Referee: Robert Whitton (4th time this season)

Easter Monday 6th April - Conference

Kidderminster Harriers 0

Bristol Rovers 3

Harrison - 50', 83', Taylor - 90'

Rovers: Puddy, Lockyer, McChrystal (Capt.), Parkes [Booked], Brown, Dawson, Mansell, Lines (Clarke - 90'), Monkhouse, Harrison (Taylor - 85'), Blissett [Booked].

Unused Substitutes: Mildenhall, Leadbitter, Clarke, Gosling.

Attendance: 4,229 inc at least 2,619 Gas.

Referee: Simon Bennett (3rd time this season)

Played 43 Points 84 Position 2nd   *Gap to leaders [Barnet] = 1 point*

Goodnight Ben

I didn't know Ben Hiscox, the Rovers fan who tragically died last week a few days after a cruel accident whilst playing for Stoke Gifford United, but I get the distinct feeling I didn't need to know him personally in order to deduce what a fine young man he was and how missed he will be by family, friends and a wide range of footballing buddies alike. I know for certain that I would not get the eulogies he received from everyone who had the privilege to know him.

The minute's applause (before the Chester match) to celebrate his life was the loudest in memory, and a spontaneous burst of 'Goodnight Irene' started up by a man just to my right on the Blackthorn Terrace, was spine-tingling to say the least. Add to this that his family and friends were at the touchline, and that the impressive hoard of Chester fans and players graciously and heartily joined in, and you won't be surprised to hear that I saw some tears being shed by grown men. After the exhilarating 5-1 thrashing Chris Lines ran over to his family to console them, and Darrell Clarke said he'd, "like to dedicate our victory to Ben and his family. It's heart-breaking when a family suffers a loss like that and it really puts things into perspective."

It is easy to be cynical about these now regular applause's, but in general they are impeccably observed, by the very people that are often dismissed by society as mindless thugs and drunks. The minute's silence a month ago for the tragically short life of Rebecca Watts was definitely the most serene stillness I have even been part of; even the normal watch beeps and incoming mobile phone calls were not to be heard. Some sporting clubs have taken to a preference for applause's rather than silences, but pure silence was definitely more respectful for that occasion, and was truly thought provoking about the fragility of young lives in our wonderful city.

It is also easy to be pessimistic about the state of modern-day football, and football fans, but we can often be a fine bunch, from the 'Fans Forum Sponsor Club' (FFSC) I wrote about last week, to the tireless work of the Bristol Rovers Supporters Club, and the generous contributions fans make to collections taken outside the ground most matches, usually in aid of local charities. We've recently had greyhounds and The Southmead Project, and of course the efforts to raise money for Oskar Pycroft's life changing operation.

On the field of play we saw the most scintillating performance of the season so far, with a 5-1 drubbing of Chester FC in front of the largest Conference crowd this season. It may sound strange given the result but I thought that Chester looked quite a handy side, especially when with the ball, which hopefully shows how good we were, and for once our finishing was quite clinical. This, plus the slick 3-1 win over Aldershot Town suggest that two more home wins are very achievable, and if we do only end up in the play-offs no team will fancy facing us at the Mem, especially with home advantage in the second leg now guaranteed.

Although we weren't playing the strongest opponents, six comfortable points and eight dynamic goals, spread around four really in-form players, are giving Gasheads real confidence that we could secure three wins, which funnily enough would give us the same W-D-L record as Gerry Francis's 1989/90 Title winning team. The problem of course is whether Barnet will slip up, as they are grinding out mediocre 1-0 wins like we were earlier in the season. They may not be impressive but they are still three points.

As always the support of thousands of Gasheads are with our team, home and away, and I hope that we can not only be gracious victors if we get the title, but also gracious losers if we 'only' achieve second or third place, with a points haul that most other seasons would have seen us get automatic promotion.

WEEK 50 - GREAT EXPECTATIONS

PUBLISHED ON FRIDAY 17TH APRIL 2015

Saturday 11th April - Conference

Bristol Rovers 2   **Southport 0**

Harrison - 11', Taylor - 50'

Rovers: Puddy, Leadbitter, McChrystal (Capt.), Parkes, Brown, Dawson (Balanta - 87'), Mansell, Lines, Monkhouse, Taylor, Harrison [Booked] (Blissett - 82' [Booked])

Unused Substitutes: Mildenhall, Leadbitter, Easter.

Attendance: 8,251 inc 117 Sandgrounders (surely one of the best nicknames ever!)

Referee: John Brooks (2nd time this season)

Played 44 Points 87 Position 2nd   *Gap to leaders [Barnet] = 1 point*

Great Expectations

In Charles Dickens' masterpiece the 'Great Expectations' of the title were the hopes and dreams of wealth, love, and becoming a gentleman, all washed down of course with the old Victorian dénouement of the eventual triumph of good over evil. For us Gasheads the original expectations for our life in the Conference weren't that great, and were surpassed a long time ago anyway.

So do we stick with the expectations that many fans had at the start of the season, such as a play-off spot with maybe a less than positive outcome, or do we really now push on and expect promotion, by whatever route we have to take?

I've never fully understood the idea that you have expectations in August that should then last you a full eight months and never change. The football squad changes during the long season, the manager and staff also often change, and the finances can ebb and flow as well depending on variables such as ownership, investment, transfers and cup matches, so why shouldn't expectations also be liquid as well?

I'm not suggesting that a brace of good games should result in an angry insurrection if a title isn't later secured, but I do think that after sustained success on the pitch we should be allowed to have escalating aspirations and to be able to actually enjoy the wins for once. One loss in the last 27 league matches (or two losses in 37 league matches; take your pick of stats), unbeaten in 18 away matches, nine wins in the last 12 matches, and 21 clean sheets in 44 league games, are all staggering statistics which show that we shouldn't be frightened of any team in a potential play-off, and should be plotting a path for promotion this season rather than harking back to our poor start, or our occasional slip ups to a couple of relatively local clubs famed for their rich owners rather than their Football League history.

No team in their right minds would wish to face us at the moment, and we not only have a far stronger and improved squad than the one that started the season, but one that is playing with confidence, mutual understanding, and some considerable flair and goal threat.

Does this, or our steadfast fan base, guarantee us promotion? Of course not, but it gives us a great platform to have the confidence (not arrogance), that we can grasp the reward that being one of the top two teams in the league warrants. We aren't Luton Town in 2010 and hopefully won't freeze like them either. We have learnt very fast how to adapt to life after the Football League, especially when faced with early defeats, and negativity. And one little known fact is that in their first four seasons in the Conference, Luton Town consistently failed in the league against the top five teams, a fragility which was re-iterated by three consecutive play-off losses.

Paul Buckle famously said that Gasheads needed to lower their expectations after the poor start to our first season back in the basement division in 2011, and to some degree he was right, but primarily only in regards to the impatience of our expectations rather than the actual League One vision itself. One day I will write a re-appraisal of the orange coloured one, but not quite yet. Rather like the life and times of Muammar Gaddafi in Libya or Mohamed Siad Barre in Somalia, the wounds are still a little too raw.

What matters to me is that our Great Expectations are firmed based on reality and our new approach. Just as exactly 75% of Conference Premier football clubs were founded in the Victorian era of benevolence, gentlemanly conduct, and hard work, it is important that our aspirations to improve are not driven by arrogance or snobbery, or flashing cash at players coming for an easy ride, but through the timeless conviction of education, discipline, and respect.

For Dickens his novel was a 'homecoming' back to previous themes and territory after an anguished divorce; half comfort blanket, half rallying cry to buck ourselves up and get back to basics. A homecoming of our own would certainly be a fitting tribute to loyal Gasheads, and rather like Dickens's protagonist, Pip, we, 'the Rovers', may often be outcasts, weighed down by our less than glorious past, but there is no reason why we cannot build on this excellent turnaround in moral fibre and achieve our own 'walking off into the sunset' moment.

WEEK 51 - THE COMPANY OF STRANGERS

PUBLISHED ON THURSDAY 23RD APRIL 2015

Saturday 18th April - Conference

Dover Athletic 1   **Bristol Rovers 1**

Modeste - 88'   Harrison - 64'

Rovers: Puddy, Lockyer, McChrystal (Capt.) [Booked], Parkes, Brown, Mansell, Monkhouse, Lines, Harrison (Balanta - 76'), Taylor, Blissett.

Unused Substitutes: Mildenhall, Leadbitter, Gosling, Baggie.

Attendance: 2,351 inc 1,562 Gas.   Referee: Craig Hicks (2nd time this season)

Played 45 Points 88 Position 2nd   *Gap to leaders [Barnet] = 1 point*

The Company of Strangers

We matched the all-time Conference Premier record of 19 unbeaten away games in a row on Saturday, but it is a completely hollow 'achievement' after metaphorically snatching defeat from the jaws of victory. I've witnessed four away draws this season. If we had instead won two and lost two of those games we wouldn't possess that unbeaten record but we would be top of the league. 16 stalemates, 12 of them away, may really cost us this season, and two of them have come from late Dover Athletic equaliser's.

Indeed it was the perfect trip to remind myself of my friends blog 'Go Mad or Stop Caring' where Matthew Foster, nudged by 'the wife', often ends up evaluating his away day as 'a good day out ~~ruined~~ slightly stained by 90 minutes of football'.

Some will say that a draw at the sloping pitch of a team with the fifth best home record in the league is not a bad day, but it really was a must-win, and the expectations of Gasheads obviously rose when we were one up and Barnet were faced with the opposite circumstances.

Any regular reader of my analysis will know I have consistently supported Darrell Clarke from the start, but equally I'm not afraid to pipe up when I think he got it seriously wrong.

The second I got there, after a long and aspirated tramp around two rugby pitches to the away end - think Aldershot - and saw the very dry pitch, the flags reacting to a curious swirling breeze, Adam Dawson no-where to be seen and Tom Lockyer still mysteriously keeping Daniel Leadbitter out, I thought it was all wrong. Those conditions were crying out for pace and playing it on the ground, yet our line-up deliberately eschewed any fleet footedness we had, and the players hoofed it in the air. Nathan Blissett was supposed to be a third striker but it just stretched the trio too far apart across the front line, gave no central focus for our aerial balls, and left a shocking lack of width. Three up front has never worked this season and I'm not only still disappointed that it happened again, but also at the treatment Dawson, not even named in the squad for what would have been his last game on loan.

Long balls, hopeful balls, percentage balls. Quite a lot of balls. If you play like that on a parched, bobbly pitch you might as well just give up on having any tangible tactics, unless you consciously want to call that a method and take pleasure in the ball bouncing everywhere, and their lumpy centre backs winning bags of headers.

This hopeful percentage game was not only dire to watch, but more importantly was never a technique that could attempt to control a vital match. We don't play like that at home, and we haven't done that during three very impressive wins on the trot, with an aggregate score of 11-2. I don't see why we didn't pick a team to retain possession and use pace, passing and dribbling to win, just like we have for the last, very successful, 270 minutes we have played. If Dover want to play that game, fair enough, but why did we have to try to match them?

We looked in complete control after our goal, against a team visibly tiring from their considerable efforts in the first hour, but we inexplicably let them back in the game, and invited pressure with some poor clearances and weak defending. Gifting late corners to a decent home team like Dover was verging on suicidal.

I've never seen so many Gasheads leave a ground so deathly quiet. No (outward) anger, no booing. Just so, so, so disappointed not only at the result, but also the performance and both the timing and dubious legitimacy of the sickening late equaliser. Our best chance of 'success' for many, many years and we messed it up.

Fortunately the bucolic beauty of the walk back to the car tempered our disappointment; along the River Dour (dour by name, but distinguished by nature), past the exquisite Georgian Crabble Corn Mill, and finished off with a 20 minute chill out watching a cover of coots in the middle of watercourse, half being fed by daddy coot, and half being kept warm by mummy coot. As an agreeable pub pie followed and was washed down with a fresh pint of local ale, a chat with a random Gashead reminded me of the value of the company of strangers, and slowly the (blue) mist cleared from my eyes.

At this point you may be thinking I'm round the bend or indifferent but I can assure you I am still passionately annoyed at that performance. But we surely need these added extras at the majority of away days, because if we travel away expecting complete domination and a bright and breezy 200 mile journey home, we will often be setting ourselves up for a fall. If we wanted almost guaranteed 'success' we could become plastic Arsenal fans, or watch our noisy neighbours waste £65 million, only for them to finally realise, rather like we have, that an efficient manager, with carefully selected, well drilled and motivated players is actually more important than money and vanity.

So what now? Well, the weekend showed that almost anything can happen in football, and certainly that one goal is rarely enough, so we dust ourselves down and go again. As usual. Gateshead have not lost away to any of the top six teams (except us), and have scored in all but four of their 22 away games, and although they are currently decimated by injuries, the glare of the BT Sport cameras and the pressure of a gigantic crowd at the Hive could well prove harder than some pundits may think.

There will be more Gasheads at a sold-out Mem than for any home league match since 1980 and despite the relative sadness that may be prevalent come 7pm, being in with a genuine chance of top spot on the final game of the season is not an achievement to induce too much melancholy. We still have several chances to escape this place and despite the wonders of the River Dour and the Crabble area, I dearly hope that will have been our sole trip to Dover.

WEEK 52 - WE'VE GOTTA GET OUT OF THIS PLACE

PUBLISHED ON WEDNESDAY 29TH APRIL 2015

Saturday 25th April - Conference

Bristol Rovers 7   **Alfreton Town 0**

Gosling - 20', Harrison - 29',
Taylor - 45', 48', Mansell - 79',
Monkhouse - 82', Parkes - 90'

Rovers: Puddy, Lockyer (Leadbitter - 71'), McChrystal (Capt.), Parkes, Brown, Gosling, Lines (Clarke - 71'), Mansell, Monkhouse, Taylor, Harrison (Balanta - 62').

Unused Substitutes: Mildenhall, Blissett.

Attendance: 11,085 inc 97 Derbyshire Reds.   Referee: Ben Toner

Played 46 Points 91 Position 2nd   *Barnet win the title by 1 point. Well done Bees.*

We've Gotta Get Out of This Place

Although this Conference season has been an amiable sojourn for most of us Gasheads, I still have The Animals' 1965 track 'We've Gotta Get Out of This Place' ringing in my head. The single was only kept off the chart's top spot by The Beatles' 'Help!' and was also included on 'The Animals are Back' EP, two musical titles that must have resonance for long suffering Gasheads!

Just as Eric Burdon growled those words with his customary passion, I hope we will be fervently singing 'The Gas are Back' at Wembley on the 17th of May. It was hard enough being a Rovers fan when regularly towards the wrong end of League Two, without now having to whisper to people that the team you single-mindedly support are currently in the fifth tier of football.

Although Forest Green Rovers have proved to be a bit of a bogey team for us this season, and were one of only three sides we never beat in the league (Eastleigh and Dover Athletic made up that triumvirate of tribulation), we must still be the team no-one wants to face in the play-offs. We've not lost away since September, and have the best home record in the league, having won 17 out of the 23 bouts. Statistically we should therefore draw the away leg this Wednesday and win the home leg next Sunday, although I suspect they will be two tight and uncompromising games.

It is often said that the in-form team will win the play-offs. If so then any team could win it this year as the top five in the final league table are also the top five in the current form table. We are second in the form table over the last six games, whereas FGR are fourth. Even more encouragingly we are top of the form table for the last 10 games, and the 7-0 execution of poor Alfreton Town on Saturday took our minds off the failure of Barnet to slip up and hand us the title. Even though we were disappointed, at least it was a stress-free day compared to our final home game of last season, and we could enjoy, to some degree, a masterful performance on a picture perfect pitch. Such a heavy win was surprisingly morale boosting considering the bigger picture elsewhere.

As we shrewdly kept the 'away terrace' to satisfy our own demand, I was part of the 99.1% of the Mem buzzing with Gasheads. I imagine this will prove to be an amazing one-off that we will never witness as football fans again. I kept looking over to the 'away terrace', as we all often do during a game, to see it full for the first time this season (see photo on page 88). I then had to remind myself that it was full of Gas, backed by that beautiful BRFC Totaliser flag evoking memories of our spiritual home, Eastville.

There are plenty of positives going into the play-offs, including simple things such as no new injuries or suspensions, Ellis Harrison looking sharp despite being slightly injured at the Crabble, the remarkable re-emergence of Jake Gosling, the loyal faith shown in Will Puddy, and Angelo Balanta looking quite comfortable in a centre forward position when the game was even more expansive and open.

Most importantly Darrell Clarke has been there and won the 'Play Off Winner' T-shirt both times, and in very differing circumstances. In 2010/11 Clarke and Mikey Harris were thrown in the deep end after Salisbury City's financial problems and double relegation. The Whites suffered a poor finish to the league season, yet still won the play-offs, against teams in better form than them, both of whom had already beaten them during the regular season. Salisbury went through after a penalty shoot out. That experience could come in handy one day soon...

2012/13 saw the opposite mode of pressure, as they had long dominated second spot and a weight of expectation hung around their necks. The Whites kept their nerve and went through in extra time. That experience could also come in handy one day soon...

Come on Gas. Now's your chance. Please show us the way out of this place!

WEEK 53 - DEAR DALE

PUBLISHED ON TUESDAY 5TH MAY 2015

Wednesday 29th April - Conference Play-Off Semi-Final - First Leg

Forest Green Rovers 0   **Bristol Rovers 1**

Taylor - 17'

Rovers: Puddy, Lockyer, McChrystal (Capt.), Parkes, Brown, Gosling (Blissett - 81'), Mansell (Clarke - 90'), Lines, Monkhouse, Taylor, Harrison [Dismissed].

Unused Substitutes: Mildenhall, Leadbitter, Balanta.

Attendance: 3,338 inc 825 official Gas, but more unofficially, including me!

Referee: Lee Swabey (4th time this season)

Sunday 3rd May - Conference Play-Off Semi-Final - Second Leg

Bristol Rovers 2   **Forest Green Rovers 0**

Lines - 24', Taylor - 88'

Rovers: Puddy, Lockyer, McChrystal (Capt.), Parkes, Brown, Gosling, Mansell [Booked] (Clarke - 86'), Lines, Monkhouse, Taylor (Balanta - 89'), Blissett.

Unused Substitutes: Mildenhall, Leadbitter, Lucas.

Attendance: 10,563 inc 665 Forest dwellers

Referee: Darren England (also 4th time this season)

Dear Dale

As a man recognised for informality, can I call you Dale?

Ok, Dale it is.

As Chairman and majority shareholder of Forest Green Rovers I feel impassioned to write to you to offer my casual support to your club. Dependant on a few changes of course...

I may get pelted in rotten (organic) tomatoes by my fellow Gasheads for admitting this, but I think there is a lot to be admired about how your club conducts itself off the pitch. From solar panels and rainwater harvesting, to electric cars and keeping a kit for two years rather than trying to fleece fans with expensive new kits every season.

I can appreciate that recently changing the shirts and the club logo may not have gone down well with all of the Green Army (I presume you had heard about the nuclear fallout when previous directors disastrously changed the name to Stroud FC in 1989?), but as an outsider I think they are beautiful, and well designed, just like your web site. The 'FGR' moniker is also a less than hippie-ish 'branding' that has strong legs.

Even the renaming of the road into the New Lawn to 'Another Way' brought a wry smile to my fizzog. It may prove to be a pun that runs thin after a while, but I liked it. Donating any profit from the 'Park & Ride' scheme for last Wednesday's match to Nailsworth Primary School was also a touch of class that many clubs don't possess.

Your staff were polite when I encountered them, and although we will probably have to agree to disagree on the measly allocation of official match tickets you decided to give us, at least the Stewards and Police did seem to use common sense to leave peaceful Gasheads alone when they had 'infiltrated' the rather sparsely populated home areas near the away end.

As an ethical vegetarian for nearly all my adult life (and previously vegan for many years) I was actually looking forward to the food at your agreeable ground. Indeed I rarely eat at away matches as usually there is frankly nothing vegetarian available, except a bag of crisps that is probably three months past its sell by date. The freshly rolled falafel wrap was right up my street, as was the Fair Trade coffee, and all with change from £4.

As a lover of quirky proceedings at away games, I have sporadically sought out unusual routes and entrances to grounds, and the trek through a wood full of wild garlic to get to the New Lawn has inspired me to start a new blog, snappily entitled 'Football by Footpath' (reprinted after this article).

I imagine you will approve Dale, as, like you, I truly believe there is 'Another Way' in life.

Do you want the bad news now?

I was pleased to read that if you snapped your company Ecotricity in half like a stick of rock you'd see it is 'green' all the way through. It's a shame then that the word 'class' won't be running ALL the way through FGR's version of the sugary seaside snack.

I can appreciate that your primary aspiration was to 'introduce sustainability to a whole new audience - football fans', so I'm not so naïve as to think that you are necessarily fascinated by the actual game of pig's bladder itself, but as a person who has found success from being 'unconventional', it is surprising that that you hired such a conventional manager who has yet to emerge from the 1980's, when physicality and soporific hoofball reigned supreme.

They say the best way to make a multi-millionaire into a millionaire is to get him to invest in a football team. Mark my words, you will get no-where fast with Mr. Pennock at the helm, and you might bankrupt your good self to boot.

I realise that football Chairmen are probably about as welcome in the Manager's Office as a hungry lion in a tube train, but when you appointed him couldn't you have at least given Mr. Pennock some guidelines about how your ethical ethos and elegance could be continued onto the pitch?

I'm not asking for only vegans to play, or for players to offer their opposite numbers a charming bunch of red roses as they line-up, but it would be nice if several of your players, and recent ex-players, weren't utter thugs on the pitch, and convicted thugs off of it. To see these players and these negative, backward tactics at a progressive club like FGR is akin to a bad dream in which Gandhi owns shares in an arms manufacturer and Linda McCartney and Franz Kafka are 'round the back of the terraces munching on illicit bacon butties.

We gave your guys one hell of a football lesson on the pitch and you deserved it.

Give me a bell when you've got rid of your ruffians and dinosaurs, and I'd be delighted to see you as my second team and pop up to the self-styled 'little club on the hill' when time permits. Oh, and a solar powered ski-lift style contraption for that gert big 'ill would be much appreciated as well.

Yours, still puffed out,

Martin Bull

SPECIAL FEATURE

FOOTBALL BY FOOTPATH

Forest Green Rovers F.C. vs. Bristol Rovers F.C.

Conference Play-Off Semi-Final, 1ˢᵗ leg - 29ᵗʰ April 2015

The New Lawn, Another Way (oh ha. yes ha ha. I get it. ha ha ha ha ha ha ha ha. ok, enough now...), Nailsworth, Gloucestershire, GL6 0FG.

Given that Nailsworth really is a small Cotswold market town (pop: 5,794 - I almost expected that to be written in red paint on an old piece of wood like in the eerie Clint Eastwood Spaghetti Western 'High Plains Drifter') and that football fans always complain about (a) the congestion and limited parking around the top of the hill, and (b) the walk up the said hill, I decided to take the advice of Dale Vince's brilliant punning and find 'another way' to arrive. I am actually really fond of Mr. Vince (unconventional owner of Ecotricity and FGR), and it is a credit to him that this was the first 'football by footpath' I'd bothered to really think about and start writing up.

I'd never been to the ground before, having been in London on the August Bank Holiday in 2014 when we played our first ever match there and packed out two sides of the ground with 1,886 Gasheads (precisely 49.9% of the total crowd, and I bet a few who sneaked into the seats or hospitality unofficially pushed it over the 50% mark).

There are quite literally no pubs near the ground, with the nearest being down at the bottom of the hill, in the town itself. Or are there...? A quick gander at an OS map and brief reconnoitre down some steep side roads on the way back from my trip to utterly, totally, unashamedly blag the right to buy some tickets for the virtually empty 'home' terrace (the whole story is far too long to write down - 10 minutes of slightly unproductive duplicity hinged purely on two little words I threw into the mix) confirmed that there was a great parking spot and little old pub not that far from the ground, and certainly within a woodland walk that would suit 'football by footpath'.

For more 'football by footpath' adventures please visit
http://footballbyfootpath.blogspot.co.uk

But surely everyone else had also stopped whinging about pubs and parking by now and done a tad of searching on the Internet as well? Hadn't they? Obviously not, as our arrival there was greeted with the type of stares that suggested they had no idea a football ground has been within a 10-15 minute walk of them for the past 89 years.

The George Inn on Newmarket Road (GL6 0RF / Tel - 01453 833228 / Map reference ST8411499653 apparently) is an amazing pub though, especially if you like history, good beer, and out of the way locations, with pleasant views across the Miry Brook towards Shortwood thrown in for free. If you look carefully you can even see the new Wicker Man they are building over on the top of the hill. I personally don't mind the sight of an old one; it's the new ones I worry about. The three separate chimneys suggest the Inn was previously a row of three cottages. It apparently became a pub in 1820 and was renamed in 1910 to honour the incoming George V.

View from the pub

Considering its location up a dead end road it's hardly surprising it seems a lot like a locals pub. Tough. As long as the beer is ok I don't really care that much. They had two real ales on pump from the local Uley Brewery, plus one from the even closer Stroud Brewery, and Timothy Taylor's classic 'Landlord' from 'up north'. I believe they have Uley beers on most of the time and most probably Stroud ones as well.

The George Inn, circa 1997

The gents toilet is in a separate old building in front of the pub. We genuinely didn't realise it was there when already ensconced inside the pub, and as the barman totally blanked me when I tried to ask (a point off for that matey!) I decided to use the Ladies which was clearly signposted next to where we were sitting. It is upstairs though and presumably is also the bathroom for B&B guests or live-in staff as it contained shaving materials, shower gel, and everything you would need for a bath and ablutions. Or maybe they shave the locals here, or even worse, the outsiders. My friends (a Canary and a Bluebird) remarked about a quirk in the bath itself, which drained from an exit in the middle of the tub. Well, they do do things a bit funny like in Gloucestershire. BTW - I am legally allowed to make such jokes by the West Country Bumpkin Act of 1752 as I was born within 800 metres of the Gloucestershire / Somersetshire / Wiltshire 'Three Shires' border crossing, near Colerne, and have had an identity crisis ever since.

When you come out of The George head to your right, up the main road. Ignore any roads to your left and right, until you come to a clear fork in the narrow road. Stay right (the appropriately entitled Wood End Lane), carry on until the road finishes and you'll find a little footpath that leads you onto the dirt path that heads up through High Wood and to the back of the ground. If for any reason you accidentally veered left at the fork, you will simply reach the end of that particular road, and after a few minutes will join up with the same public footpaths that lead up the hill. Basically all paths lead up the steep hill (a 65 metre elevation from the pub), and straight to the ground. You can't really go that wrong. Honestly. It may seem disconcerting to the average football fan, but trust me, I am a ticket blagging liar who will pretend my father was an FGR fan from Coaley in order to get tickets. Just keep on going up and up!

At this point I am reminded of the 'turtle' story. Its origin dates back to at least the mid 19th Century, and although versions now wildly vary about who tells the story, all versions go along the same lines. After a talk on cosmology and the structure of the solar system by a clever academic, a little old lady in the hall approaches the learned lecturer and informs him that his theory of the solar order is completely wrong, and that the Earth in fact rests on the back of a huge turtle. 'But, my dear lady', the Professor asks, as politely as possible, 'what holds up the turtle?'. 'Ah', she replies, 'that's easy to answer. He is standing on the back of another turtle'. 'Oh, I see', said the Professor, trying to bite his tongue, 'But would you be so good as to tell me what holds up the second turtle?'. 'It's no use, Professor', said the old lady, realising he was trying to lead her into a logical trap, 'It's turtles all the way down!'

With FGR it is hills and hills all the way up.

The scramble up through High Wood was charming, through swathes of wild garlic, although the slide back down in the pitch black was strangely more difficult. A practical man in our party had said he would bring a torch, but he clearly wasn't that practical as he failed to do so and was also still in his slick soled office flippers. He might as well have worn shoes stolen from a Ten Pin Bowling alley, or blocks of pure pig lard on his feet (Gloucester Old Spot anyone?). I bet Ray Mears doesn't have this problem, but then again Ray has no friends. Nor would you if you ate snake poo for breakfast. I rescued the day with a bright mobile phone light and Tour de France cries of 'Allez, Allez'.

Once at the top of the ascent the back of the home terrace can be spotted through a fence (this was the Trevor Horsley stand at the old Lawn before being dragged 400 metres and re-erected at the new stadium). After climbing through a broken section and emerging like three urchins from a Victorian chimney an old boy stewarding in the car park jokingly asked us, 'where have you lot come from?'. Well I assumed he was joking - it was certainly not your average way to emerge into the confines of a new-ish football ground for an important play-off match.

If you prefer to avoid an ungainly scramble through a broken fence, you can play safe and follow the fence around the west side of the ground (this also is a public footpath). This leads you up and over the famous hill where you can see part of the pitch for free, and then around to the main road and the front of the stadium.

Well Dale, thanks for giving my quirky challenge a bit of a push. In equal measures I do and I don't look forward to a return trip. If such an occasion arises just make sure it's in the Football League yeah?

'football by footpath' is my occasional blog to chart away day travels to British football grounds that use any slightly quirky method of arrival. This will usually involve a smidgen of research, a public footpath or a canal towpath, shanks' pony, a pub and preferably decent weather. Falling down hills and getting lost is also distinctly possible, but it's hardly an extreme sport, so hand glider geeks and parachutists need not apply.

Why am I happy to arrive at the back entrance via an overgrown field full of cow pats?

Well, I like thinking outside the box, or even ripping the whole box up and starting again. And as much as I love a packed football terrace INSIDE the ground, don't you sometimes prefer to avoid the modern day madding crowd outside of it and not be herded along some tedious route for away fans? There is also the bonus of being in the great British countryside, free parking or a less than obvious train station, an easier getaway, being greener, and hopefully a country pub that isn't full of sweaty Ipswich Town fans.

WEEK 54 – WHO WILL RID ME OF THIS MANSFIELD NIGHTMARE?

PUBLISHED ON TUESDAY 12TH MAY 2015

As I went to shave last Sunday at stupid o'clock in the morning, ahead of the crucial match with Forest Green Rovers, I blearily looked in the mirror and I swear I saw, amongst the steam, nine little letters appear on the glass in ghostly writing. They seemed to spell out 'Mansfield', but as I rubbed my eyes they mysteriously disappeared. Upon stumbling into the bedroom I flipped over the calendar and let out a yelp as I realised it was the 3rd of May.

Yes, it was exactly a year ago since that ill-fated day in the sunshine of 2014, when the football team I have supported for over 25 years were disgraced both on and off the pitch.

That week was also the exact moment in time I started this blog. For my opening article I was fully expecting to write a piece about how any 'celebrations' after a dull-all draw with the Stags had to be seen as pure relief, and not any endorsement of yet another dire season following the Pirates. Instead I was thrown in at the deep-end amidst a maelstrom of anger, blame, embarrassment and anxiety about the future of our once proud club.

We just can't seem to shake off the fallout from that day, and the Mansfield connections seem to follow us around like a bad smell. I dearly hope that this stench of failure, along with the whiff of fish, can be eradicated by battering Grimsby Town next weekend at Wembley.

Mansfield, Mansfield, Mansfield. I see that word in my sleep, as a I drive, as I cut the grass, even as I slake my thirst for local history.

Whilst Bristol and Kingswood were famous nationwide in the mid-18th Century for the initial stages of Methodism, under John Wesley, his brother Charles, and George Whitefield, their religious tentacles spread far and wide over time, and in 1897 a certain Mansfield Town F.C. were originally formed as 'Mansfield Wesleyans'. I have asked them to pray for us next Sunday, but all I got was an 'out of office' reply. So much for a hotline to God.

As a young adult all I really knew about the town of Mansfield was that it was apparently the smallest town to have a Football League club, and that Bernard

Jewry lived there as a child. No, Jewry was not a cult centre forward you've never heard of, but he was unique in the music business for having the Cuckoo-like ability to take over not just one, but two performing personas, first as Shane Fenton, and later as glam rocker Alvin Stardust.

When thinking about born and bred Mansfieldians, I recollected that a certain Craig Disley was born nearby. One of our best attacking midfielders for many years, Dis, the ginger ... er... chap with a leap like a salmon, was surprisingly jettisoned by the defensive minded Paul Trollope after five years as a first team regular at the Mem. He is currently considered to be one of the best three players at Grimsby Town. Hmmm.

As much as I enjoyed the videos of Darrell Clarke singing like an old-time Gashead in The Vic on the Gloucester Road, the most intense of pubs local to the Mem, his opening salvo managed to send a shiver down my spine as he roared; "Listen, I was brought up on a rough Council estate in Mansfield...". My backbone went cold as my inner statto squawked in my ear; 'Darrell James Clarke. Born 16th December 1977, Mansfield, Nottinghamshire. Played almost 200 games for his home town club.'

Little was made of this connection when it was the Stags that we faced a year ago in front of 10,594 fans, and wearing our kit! I somehow expected Darrell to be able to pull out a few special favours for us, although I then had to stop that train of thought after recalling the 1963 match fixing scandal that saw Esmond Million and Keith Williams banned from football for life. It was in fact Mansfield Town's Brian Phillips who fatefully approached Million, leading him and fellow Stag Sammy Chapman to not only be banned for life, but also thrown in jail.

So how fitting it was that a crowd of 10,563 saw a rejuvenated Rovers side slickly outmanoeuvre Forest Green Rovers to earn a tilt at redemption. Wags may suggest that the missing 31 fans were those still banned from the ground for their bad loser conduct the year previous. Sadly we aren't alone in such shock relegations, nor shocking behaviour, as in 2008 Mansfield Town were also sent down to non-league via a 1-0 loss at the last home game of the season, amidst ugly scenes directed at the controversial then owner Keith Haslam. A young Nathan Arnold (who incidentally scored his first ever career goal against Rovers) was on the Stags side that day, alongside a less than young Jefferson Louis.

Thinking of strikers, pony tailed Ollie Palmer is currently on fire for Grimsby alongside Arnold, and guess which team he is on loan from? Yes, you worked it out. His strike rate in a brace of years for the Stags is only a goal in every nine games, yet he's been a revelation at the Mariners, with a goal every two games. The good news for us is that he's just been offered a new contract by Mansfield so complacency may have some effect next week.

Whilst this season has restored our faith in many of the positive attributes of Bristol Rovers, the job isn't completed yet. For these Mansfield nightmares to be truly put to bed we will need to win the Conference Play-Off Final at Wembley next week.

Nothing else is acceptable to begin to bleach this stain out of our history.

Come on Gas!

QI STATS - SIMPLY THE BEST *
* it was in non-league though

- ☠ WINS = 25 - best season since 1989/90 (Third Tier, 26 wins)

- ☠ LOSES = 5 - joint lowest ever (1989/90 - Third Tier = also 5 losses)

- ☠ POINTS = 91 - second highest ever (1989/90 - Third Tier = 93)

- ☠ HOME WINS = 17 - joint best ever (with three other seasons, the last being 1972/73)

- ☠ AWAY LOSSES = 3 - lowest ever

- ☠ AWAY DRAWS = 12 - highest ever

- ☠ AWAY GAMES WITHOUT DEFEAT = 20 - highest ever - this run was extended for two extra games at the start of the 2014/15 season

- ☠ GOALS CONCEDED = 34 - second lowest ever (1973/74 - Third Tier = 33 goals)

- ☠ GOALS CONCEDED AT HOME = 14 - best since 1984/85 (Third Tier, 13 goals)

- ☠ GOAL DIFFERENCE = +39 - best since 1952/53 (Third Division South - +46)

Top to bottom –
1) Chris Power, Nick, Eddie & Aimee at the Green Man pub before the dramatic play off final win. 2) Paul Jerred's mob & some of the CE Sabadell guys, also at the Green Man. 3) Splendid bunch of Gasheads at the world's most popular pub. 4) Dan Finn's troupe outside Wembley. 5) 61 Wembley tickets for the London Gas gang.

Photos kindly supplied by –
1 = Chris Power / 2 = Paul Jerred / 3 = Alecia Benjamin / 4 = Dan Finn & Family / 5 = Via Nick Rippington but it belongs to Steve Western I believe.

Above – Robert Farquhar's beautiful panorama of Wembley
Below – Alecia Benjamin brilliantly captured the electric atmosphere at the Green Man pub before the game.

Clockwise from top left –
1) Wembley Way with hardly any black & white in sight. 2) Good to see some supporters try to make a point at the overblown prices, which were far more than for the JPT Final. 3) Fair play to this stylish mariner, who looks the business in his dapper suit. 4) Even the coppers are closet Gasheads. 5) Josh Hazard with possibly the biggest flag a six year old has ever held.

Photos kindly supplied by –
1 & 2 = Rick Weston /
3 = @partizanbristle / 4 = Alecia Benjamin / 5 = Dan Hazard.

Clockwise from top left – 1) Mat and Gayle Bennett, with Vaughan, Beatrice, & Honey in the baby pouch & ear defenders – surely the youngest Gashead at Wembley, aged just 4 weeks & 5 days! 2) Charlie Finn attempting the world record for massive hotdog eating. 3) Robert Oxley & grandson Thomas Oxley-Reed looking blissfully happy. 4) Haydn Vaulters & Nick Rippington growing old disgracefully. 5) Colin, Rich & Mary Clark – You may recognise Colin as the cover boy pin-up on 'Away The Gas'. 6) Julie & Mike Jay, with expert Rovers historian Mr.Jay in what seems to be a shirt signed by Luke Basford! Now that is real history.

Photos kindly supplied by – 1 = Mat Bennett / 2 = Dan Finn / 3 = Kelly Oxley-Reed / 4 = Nick Rippington / 5 = Rich Clark / 6 = Mike Jay

Above – Flying the flag for the Pirates (photo by Maki Toad)
Below – The anxiety is lifted and three tiers of Gas can relax and enjoy (photo by Rick Weston)

Above & Right – Re-live the game through the lenses of Alecia Benjamin (large photo, & small photos 3 & 6) and Rick Weston (small photos 1,2,4 & 5). The line-up, the huddle, Matty Taylor getting booked instead of a pen, relief at Ellis's equaliser, THAT substitution, watching the pens, and finally Manse's winning pen just about to hit the net!

Clockwise from top left –
1) The players almost merge into the crowd amidst a sea of blue & white.
2) In DC I trusted. Top man.
3) The moment the cup was lifted (via the big screen!)
4) They deserved to be on that gantry. 91 points. Only a handful of losses. No away loss since September.
5) Sometimes I need this photo to remind me it was real! We really did win the final.
6) 'Scenes' in the crowd, presumably with a shift lens style 'toy town' effect added.

Photos kindly supplied by – 1, 5 & 6 = @partizanbristle / 2 & 4 = Rick Weston / 3 = Maki Toad.

Clockwise from top left – 1) One of my favourite players for a long time, Lee Brown, deservedly gets his turn with the trophy. 2) Genuinely the most bizarre sight I have EVER witnessed at football. 3) If the famous Che Guevara photo can sell 150 million T-shirts, just think what THIS iconic stance could achieve.
4) Open top bus parade through the more desirable parts of Bristol.
5) Steve Yates hasn't jumped like that since 1996.

Photos kindly supplied by – 1 & 5 = Rick Weston /
2 & 3 = Me (Martin Bull) / 4 = Dan Lovering.

WEEK 55 - WE'VE GOT OUR ROVERS BACK

PUBLISHED ON SATURDAY 23RD MAY 2015

Sunday 17th May - Conference Play-Off Final

Bristol Rovers 1

Grimsby Town 1

Harrison - 29'

John-Lewis - 2'

Penalties

Chris Lines - Scored (1-0)	Craig Disley - Scored (1-1)
Matty Taylor - Scored (2-1)	Lennell John-Lewis - Scored (2-2)
Lee Brown - Scored (3-2)	Jon-Paul Pittman - Missed (3-2)
Angelo Balanta - Scored (4-2)	Craig Clay - Scored (4-3)
Lee Mansell - Scored (5-3)	

(After Extra Time) Rovers win 5-3 on pens

Rovers: Puddy [Booked] (Mildenhall - 119'), Lockyer, McChrystal (Capt.), Parkes, Brown, Gosling (Balanta - 75'), Mansell, Lines, Monkhouse, Taylor [Booked], Harrison (Blissett - 80').

Unused Substitutes: Leadbitter, Clarke.

Attendance: 47,029   Referee: Ross Joyce (3rd time this season)

We've got our Rovers back

Get in! We managed the almost unmanageable; an instant return to the Football League, and whilst I think the whole experience and total change of ethos is the best thing that has happened to the club for several decades, there is also sheer relief that such a long and nerve splitting season is finally over, and that our solitary goal has actually been achieved. As the boxer Floyd Mayweather Jnr. said, "winners win, losers have excuses", and too many times in the past we've been giving excuses for failure. No one 'deserves' success; you have to make it.

The play-off finals have actually been incredibly fair so far. All eight of the highest league finishers are playing at Wembley this season, after no finalist lost either of their play-off legs, and although some Grimsby Town fans were gutted that they lost in a cruel way, think how we've been feeling. We played 46 games, spread over eight long months, in all different weathers place. In any other league that would have given us an easy promotion. But for this league the results are thrown out the window and we had to hold our nerve three more times, especially against Grimsby who could easily have won it in the first half, or even on the vagaries of those few kicks at goal. I'm pretty sure no-one could suggest that us losing on penalties would have been a fairer end to the season.

With 193 Football League seasons jointly behind them, this match, backed by a Conference Play-Off record 47,029 fans, seemed more like a League Two or even League One final. Sadly all that was at stake was a return to a League that Gasheads had never seen before the dawn of this Millennium, and loyal Mariners had only seen for eight seasons. Both teams have been punching far below their historic weight for far too much of the last 15 years.

Conceding the first goal was hardly a surprise considering we had also done so in all four of our previous Football League Trophy and Play-Off Finals. Indeed, the Fishmens's second minute poach, and our equaliser 20 minutes or so later, had me reaching for my League Two 2006/7 Play-off Final DVD, such was the level of déjà vu that hit us in that frantic first half an hour.

As more and more players looked drained during the extra 30 minutes it looked like Daniel Leadbitter's pace was going to be introduced on the right hand side. But the moment passed and as Chris Lines went down several times with cramp, Ollie Clarke was now seen stripped off and standing next to the Fourth Official. The switch never happened and when Ollie finally sat back down it seemed clear that Darrell was holding back his final change for any potential penalty shoot out, with Lines high up the list of takers and determined to stay on the pitch in the absence of Ellis Harrison, one of our best dead ball finishers.

Finally the moment really did arrive, as Darrell van Gaal swapped goalkeepers, just as The Netherlands did against Costa Rica in last summer's World Cup Quarter Final. Thankfully Steve Mildenhall didn't engage in any of Tim Krul's cross histrionics, and although unlike Krul he didn't save a penalty, maybe it was his generously proportioned presence that contributed to the only miss of the spot-kicks, by Jon-Paul Pittman?

The change was probably mind games as much as anything else as not only did Mildenhall have form, but that previous was with the Cleethorpe's massive. Mildy was the Mariners stopper back in the 2006 League Two Play-off Final against John Ward's Cheltenham Town, and that day saved Grant McCann's penalty in normal time.

The shoot out was surprisingly uncomplicated for us, aided by the mental strength shown by our guys, not least Matty Taylor who had missed his penalty at Blundell Park on Valentine's Day, in front of the exact same keeper who faced him now, just 18 yards away. Lee Brown also stepped up to the plate, with the only Rovers penalty to send the keeper the wrong way.

The vastly under-rated Brown has shown true grit before. He missed his last penalty for Rovers, at Lincoln City back in September, when he could have won the game with his 88th minute spot kick. Did he let his momentary despair affect his attitude that day? No, as within two minutes he had a shot saved, and then supplied the cross that Ellis Harrison used to really win the game for Rovers, one of nine marvellous assists this season from the hugely reliable and loyal full back.

Those penalties, and coming back from an early battering, summed up why we won promotion.

Although Ian Holloway's post-match comment that the result had "given us our team back" has received most of the media coverage, it was actually his pre-match interview on BT Sport that gave a more coherent explanation of our footballing transformation, when he remarked that Darrell Clarke's management had "given us our attitude back".

It was this attitude, this change of ethos, that won us promotion. The win on the pitch was just football; 22 men of very similar ability kicking a pig's bladder around. But it has been the attitude of the manager, and the squad he has recruited, that has made us proud this season, and on the pitch has given us our Rovers back. A humble attitude, a hungry attitude, a disciplined attitude, a winning attitude.

Priceless.

thanks non-league teams & fans for your hospitality, but never again please Rovers...

187

EPILOGUE

Well, what a season.

One of Elmore Leonard's rules for writing was, "You are allowed no more than two or three [exclamation marks] per 100,000 words of prose." Hopefully after about 60,000 words this is a fair place to use another one to exclaim **THEY DID IT!**

In years to come we may well be looking back and not only wincing at how narrow the margin of success was and what might have happened if a few pens had gone the other way (for every BRFC great escape there is a Stockport County, a Lincoln City and a Southport), but more importantly we may well be concluding that the change in ETHOS that relegation prompted was the best thing that happened to us for many, many years. In fact without relegation we may have been motoring on regardless down Arrogant Avenue or Brainless Boulevard.

I am not proud of everything I do or say in life, but I am very satisfied that I backed DC when many others didn't and that he came through as a winner. As usual.

The list of things that irked me about a season in the fifth tier is as long at Mr. Tickle's arm (I am at heart a grumpy chap, but thankfully with a sense of humour... usually) and what annoyed me most was summed up by my thoughts in week 12 on page 31. "Darrell achieved two promotions in three seasons as a player-manager with Salisbury City, and did very well in several Cup competitions, so I've been surprised to see this labelled a tin pot achievement by some... Success is never a gimme at any level of the football pyramid and ... surely what really matters is that he DID actually achieve this success, and that many of the managerial responsibilities he obviously coped with well at The Whites, such as recruitment, contracts, training sessions, tactics, fitness, motivation, research, human dynamics, and his own relationship with his Board of Directors, will, to some degree, be similar at any level of football. A winner is a winner at any altitude."

DC may, like myself, be a bit of a prickly character at times, but how many more promotions does this guy need to deliver before people give his principled approach the respect it deserves? Please encourage him and our team whilst they endeavour to put this ethos into practice; patience is a virtue and all that...

I hope you enjoyed the book. Please send any comments / feedback to me at hello@awaythegas.org.uk and I hope you'll find time to contribute to the forthcoming 'Twerton Delight' book (see page 74).

Take care & UTG!   Martin Bull

Gas on Tour - Away Game Statistics - 2014/15

Club	Official Total of Gasheads	Total Crowd	Miles (one way, from Bristol)	Other QI Factors AT = All Ticket / SO = Sold Out / BTS = Live on BT Sport
Barnet	663	2,027	126	Tuesday night
Altrincham	376	1,463	158	
Forest Green Rovers	1,886	3,781	43	AT – Bank Holiday Monday – BTS
Braintree Town	565	1,621	177	
Lincoln City	211	2,933	182	AT
Southport	367	1,202	187	
Eastleigh	994	2,621	76	AT – Tuesday night
Aldershot Town	1,255	3,466	96	
Dorchester Town (FA Cup)	1,139	1,909	62	
AFC Telford Utd	895	2,860	118	
Tranmere Rovers (FA Cup)	340	3,559	118	
Alfreton Town	315	880	153	Tuesday night
Chester	479	2,936	180	
Wrexham	193	2,608	162	Tuesday night
Welling United	651	1,176	130	
Torquay United	1,145	3,755	97	AT – Boxing Day – No trains running
Nuneaton Town	926	1,661	112	Sunday afternoon
Woking	1,869	3,853	110	Estimated 200–300 Gas locked out!
Dartford	788	1,832	149	AT
Grimsby Town	326	4,073	232	AT
Gateshead	667	1,668	295	
FC Halifax Town	668	2,248	205	
Macclesfield Town	782	2,591	153	Originally AT, but later relaxed – BTS – Early KO (12.30pm)
Kidderminster Harriers	2,619	4,229	77	AT for all fans – SO for Gas
Dover Athletic	1,562	2,351	196	AT for all fans
FGR (Play-off)	825	3,336	43	AT for all fans – SO for Gas
TOTAL	**22,506**	**66,519**	**3,704**	

THANKS & ACKNOWLEDGEMENTS

- Many thanks to James McNamara at the Bristol Post who wrote the foreword to this book, gave me the opportunity to publish my weekly articles on their web site, and was supportive and encouraging throughout. There is no way I would have continued for over a year, nor put so much effort into them, if they weren't being seen by the public each week.

- Special thanks to my brother Chris and my best friend Mike, who often gave positive feedback and encouragement as I crawled along week after week, trying to think of new angles and vaguely entertaining topics.

- Thanks to all the Gasheads who offered me the use of their photographs to brighten up the book. The ones used in the book were supplied by Alecia Benjamin, Mat Bennett, Rich Clark, Russ Church, Colin Emmitt, the Fan's Forum Sponsor Club, Robert Farquhar, Dan Finn & family, Matthew Foster, Maki Fukuoka, Joe GasHead Esq., Dan Hazard, Mike Jay, Paul Jerred, David Johnson, Mark Lewis, Dan Lovering (@LedburyGas), Tom Meadowcroft (@partizanbristle), Kelly Oxley-Reed, Ashley Perry, Chris Power, Nick Rippington, Steve Western, Rick Weston, Karen Whitlow, Sean Williams (Sean Clevedon Gas), Wendi Williams & Simon Wilton. Phew. Now breathe...

- Thanks to Sam Martin @ TU Ink, who has efficiently handled all the print brokerage on my books, including this one.

- A general thanks to all the Gas forums, and their administrators / moderators (a truly thankless task if there ever was one!), who played a part in this book just by their very existence. It would have been hard for me to get in touch with so many interested Gasheads and photo contributors without such outlets for publicity and messages.

- Well done to all the Gasheads and Pirates who stuck with the team, and our excellent young manager, whilst they played in the lowest level of football seen for almost 100 years, and got beaten in towns even a satnav would struggle to find.

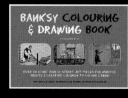

ABOUT THE AUTHOR

MARTIN BULL BECAME A GASHEAD IN 1989 AND IMMEDIATELY FELL IN LOVE WITH TWERTON PARK, STANDING NEAR G PILLAR. HAVING BEEN EXILED FOR MUCH OF HIS PAST, AWAY GAMES HAVE ALWAYS BEEN SPECIAL FOR HIM, SO MUCH SO THAT IN 2014 HE COLLECTED AND EDITED THE AWAY DAY EXPERIENCES OF OVER 40 FELLOW PIRATES FOR THE ACCLAIMED BOOK, 'AWAY THE GAS'.

HE STILL ENJOYS WRITING A WEEKLY-ISH (YES, IT HAS SLIPPED A BIT...) ONLINE ARTICLE FOR THE BRISTOL POST NEWSPAPER, ENTITLED 'G IS FOR GAS'.

IN 2006 HE WAS THE FIRST TO OFFER (FREE) TOURS AROUND LONDON'S MOST ARTY STREETS AND WROTE, PHOTOGRAPHED AND PUBLISHED THE FIRST INDEPENDENT BOOK ABOUT THE ARTIST BANKSY.

HE'S BEEN INVOLVED IN PUBLICATIONS ON AND OFF FOR OVER 20 YEARS BUT THAT BOOK WAS HIS FIRST FULLY PUBLISHED WORK. IT BECAME A DIY FAVOURITE ALL OVER THE WORLD AND IS ON ITS 5TH EDITION IN THE UK AND 2ND EDITION IN THE USA. A KOREAN VERSION APPARENTLY EXISTS BUT HE HAS NEVER SEEN IT; RATHER LIKE A GOAL BY STEVE YATES. A MAJESTIC VOLUME 2 WAS RELEASED IN 2010 AND OTHER BOOKS HAVE RECENTLY FOLLOWED, INCLUDING SHAMELESSLY JUMPING ON THE ADULT COLOURING BAND WAGON WITH AN INNOVATIVE 'BANKSY COLOURING & DRAWING BOOK'. PLEASE BUY IT BECAUSE HE'S SKINT.

MARTIN HAS DONATED £34,723 SO FAR TO CHARITIES THROUGH SALES OF HIS BANKSY BOOKS AND RELATED FUNDRAISING INITIATIVES, AND HOPES TO BE ABLE TO ADD MORE IN THE FUTURE.

PLEASE FEEL FREE TO CONTACT HIM VIA TWITTER (@AWAYTHEGAS) OR EMAIL – HELLO@AWAYTHEGAS.ORG.UK

Front cover photos by kind permission of Alecia Benjamin (Gasheads at the Green Man pub) and Rick Weston (the amazing Lee Brown lifting the cup at Wembley). Eccentric 'Full of Gas' vision by Martin Bull.

Rear cover photos (clockwise) by kind permission of Russ Church ('The Beard' with Cameron & Evie Church, & Oscar Lewis), Matthew Foster (Director parking at Braintree Town), Dan Lovering (open top bus parade) and Kelly Oxley-Reed (her father Robert Oxley & son Thomas Oxley-Reed looking blissfully happy at Wembley).

Inside cover photo of the Conference Play-Off Final at Wembley in May 2015 by kind permission of Rick Weston – possibly the easiest 'Spot The Ball' competition ever.